A Wiccan's Guide to
Prophecy and Divination

Also by Gerina Dunwich

A Wiccan's Guide to Prophecy and Divination

GERINA DUNWICH

A Citadel Press Book
Published by Carol Publishing Group

A Citadel Press Book
Published by Carol Publishing Group
Citadel Press is a registered trademark of Carol Communications, Inc.

Editorial, sales and distribution, and rights and permissions inquiries should
be addressed to Carol Publishing Group, 120 Enterprise Avenue, Secaucus, N.J.
07094.

In Canada: Canadian Manda Group, One Atlantic Avenue, Suite 105, Toronto,
Ontario M6K 3E7

Carol Publishing Group books may be purchased in bulk at special discounts for
sales promotion, fund-raising, or educational purposes. Special editions can
be created to specifications. For details, contact Special Sales Department,
Carol Publishing Group, 120 Enterprise Avenue, Secaucus, N.J. 07094.

MANUFACTURED IN THE UNITED STATES OF AMERICA
10 9 8 7 6 5 4 3 2 1

Library of Congress Cataloging-in-Publication Data

The Cataloging Data for this publication can be obtained from the Library of
Congress.

To my Mother and to Al Jackter, as always . . .
Blessed be.

Cosmic Oracle

Cosmic oracle of the shrine
uttering prophecies of the divine.
With mystical eyes iridescent
you see into the future,
the past, and the present.

Some call you a madman,
a devil, a magician.
They fear and do not understand
the power of your visions.

Cosmic oracle
mysterious and wise,
you have lived a thousand lives.
And when your life in this world ends,
your soul will be reborn again.

—from *Circle of Shadows*
by Gerina Dunwich

(US Library of Congress)

Introduction

Divination is the art and practice of obtaining knowledge of the future or of secret things by means of omens, organized systems, or prophecy. These methods provide the three main categories into which nearly all divination can be classified.

Omens are accidental or chance signs which, when properly interpreted, are believed to reveal the future, warn of impending danger, and so forth. The word "omen" derives from the Latin *ominosus*, which means "foreboding evil;" however, not all omens are necessarily of an evil nature. They can also signify such things as good fortune, love, or the birth of a child.

Divination by organized systems includes (but is in no way limited to) astrology, cards, dice, lot casting, the *I Ching*, palmistry, numerology, and the reading of tea leaves.

Many of the systematized methods were devised by the ancient Chaldeans, Babylonians, Romans, Greeks, and Chinese.

They were used by priests, shamans, and diviners not only for determining the future course of events, but also for solving problems, identifying the guilty, resolving disputes, and locating lost persons, objects, and even buried treasure.

The third and most sacred form of divination is prophecy, which relies on direct communication with divine beings or entities of the spirit world to gain insight into the future, the present, or the past. This is accomplished usually through visions (including dreams), trance states, and possession.

Under the category of prophecy are predictions made by prophets, oracles, channelers, spiritualist mediums, and any woman, man, or child who "utters by divine inspiration" or who acts as a revealer of the will of the gods.

The mystical art of divination has been practiced in one form or another since ancient times, in all levels of culture. In modern times, it is an essential part of modern Witchcraft and the nature religion of Wicca appearing in the form of crystal gazing (a Samhain tradition, also known as scrying), Tarot card interpretation, love divination, or other methods.

Many Wiccans are in favor of performing a divination of some kind prior to casting magickal spells, especially those spells which may be considered to be manipulative in nature (such as certain love spells). The purpose is to discover whether or not the outcome of the spell will have negative or positive effects. If the divination reveals that something bad or harmful will arise out of it, that particular spell is avoided or altered in such a way that its outcome will not in any way violate the Wiccan Rede, the main tenet of Wicca, which states: "An it harm none, do what thou wilt." (No Wiccan in his or her right mind wants to go against the Wiccan Rede, even unintentionally, and then have to deal with the threefold bad karma that such an action inevitably produces.)

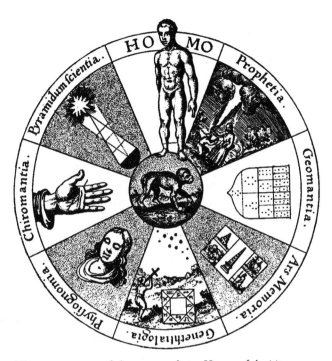

The various arts of divination, from *History of the Microcrosm*
by Robert Fludd, seventeenth century.

The numerous methods of divination included in this book
range from the ancient to the modern, and are arranged in alphabetical order for the convenience of the reader. Nearly every
form of the divinatory arts can be found within the pages of this
book.

Many of the most archaic and taboo forms of divination involved such practices as animal and human sacrifice, the conjuring of demons and spirits of the dead, urination, and torture.
Most of these were popular practices among the diviners of ancient Rome and Greece, but, luckily, they are no longer in use

in modern times. Such practices are listed in this book mainly for their historic significance, and they include anthropomancy, armomancy, cephalomancy, demonomancy, haruspicy, hemomancy, hepatoscopy, hieromancy, necromancy, ordeals, spatalamancy, splanchomancy, sternomancy, and uromancy.

Among the methods most popular with twentieth-century practitioners of divination are aleuromancy (fortune cookies), apantomancy, astragalomancy and astragyromancy (dice casting), astrology (including astro-divination and horoscopy), auramancy (the reading of auras), bibliomancy, cartomancy (especially tarotology), cheiromancy (palmistry, including cheirognomy), dowsing, graphology (handwriting analysis), lot casting, numerology, oneiromancy (dream interpretation), pendulum divination, podomancy, psychography, psychometry, scrying (gazing, especially crystallomancy), and tasseography (the reading of tea leaves).

To receive free information regarding astrological natal charts and Tarot card, palmistry and numerology readings by mail, please send a self-addressed stamped envelope to: Gerina Dunwich, P.O. Box 525, Fort Covington, New York, 12937.

BLESSED BE!

A Wiccan's Guide to Prophecy and Divination

𝕬

ABACOMANCY The art and practice of divination by reading omens in patterns of dust (possibly including the ashes of the dead).

The origin and precise method of this unusual form of divination is unknown; however, like most of the divinatory methods covered in this book, abacomancy most likely dates back to ancient times.

AERIMANCY (see AEROMANCY)

AEROMANCY (also spelled aerimancy) The art and practice of divination by the air, the winds, and various atmospheric phenomena such as spectral formations, comets, the shapes of clouds, and so forth.

This method of divination, which reaches beyond the scope of weather prognostication, dates back to the earliest of times and was practiced by diviners around the world in one form or another.

Aeromancy, in the most precise sense of the word, covers mainly the art and practice of divination by a current of air; however, in medieval times, divination by nearly any phenomenon of the heavens became classified under the title of aeromancy. In modern times, it continues to be used for primitive weather forecasting, among other things.

ALECTOROMANCY (see ALECTRYOMANCY)

ALECTROMANCY (see ALECTRYOMANCY)

ALECTRYOMANCY (also known as alectoromancy and alectromancy) The art and practice of divination involving a
rooster or a black hen. A circle, which is divided into twenty-
six equal pie-shaped parts, is drawn on the ground. Each part of
the circle represents a different letter of the alphabet and contains a wheat seed or grain of corn. After the appropriate
prayers and magickal incantations are recited, the rooster or hen
(often with its claws cut off or tied together) is placed in the
center of the circle and allowed to eat. The letter from each part
of the circle where it picks up a seed or grain is recorded and
then used to spell out a divinatory message.

It is said that this method of divination works best when the
Moon is positioned in the sign of the Ram (Aries) or the sign
of the Lion (Leo).

Another version of alectryomancy consists of reciting the
letters of the alphabet at dawn and then writing down the ones
that are said at the same time the crowing of a rooster is heard.

These methods of divination are popular throughout Africa
where they are believed to have originated.

ALEUROMANCY The art and practice of divination by messages baked inside special cakes or cookies which are then selected at random.

The origin of aleuromancy can be traced back to China,
where it was performed in ancient times for men and women
of great nobility. To gain a better understanding of what the
future held in store, the diviner would choose from an assort-
ment of special tea cakes into which tiny essays based on
philosophical tenets were baked. Upon breaking open the

tea cake, the message contained within would be revealed and interpreted.

In Europe, aleuromancy is responsible for the old custom of baking a cake containing a coin of silver. According to the tradition, the person who receives the piece of cake with the coin is either blessed with an abundance of good luck throughout the ensuing year or entitled to have one secret wish granted.

In ancient Greece, small pieces of paper containing various messages were rolled up in small balls of flour, mixed up nine times, and then given to those who desired to know their destiny. This particular form of divination was ruled by the god Apollo (one of the epithets of Apollo was aleuromancy).

The ancient practice of divination by messages baked in small balls of flour continues to be practiced in modern times in the form of fortune cookies.

ALOMANCY   The art and practice of divining future events by interpreting the symbolic patterns made by the sprinkling of salt.

Another method involves casting a handful of salt into a fire and then interpreting whatever omens may appear in the flames.

The old and well-known superstition that spilling salt brings bad luck, and that a pinch of salt sprinkled over the left shoulder averts the misfortune, most likely stems from the ancient practice of alomancy, which is also known as "halomancy."

ALPHITOMANCY   The ancient art and practice of divination to identify a guilty person by using a leaf of barley or a special barley cake that can be ingested only by persons who are innocent. If a man or woman accused of a particular crime falls ill in any way (or even if his or her stomach rumbles) after swallowing a bite of the barley cake, it is an indication of guilt.

This old method of divination is also known as critomancy, and is similar to the art and practice of crithomancy, which is divination by grain or corn.

AMNIOMANCY   The art and practice of divination by observation of the caul on a child's head at the time of birth. (A caul is a fetal membrane that covers the head of some infants at the time of their birth.)

The ancient Romans believed that when a child was born with a caul, it was an omen of phenomenal good luck. In certain parts of the world, it was believed that a person born with a caul naturally possessed second sight, could never be bewitched, and would never die by drowning.

A lead-colored caul is believed to be an omen of great misfortune for the child; a red one reveals that the child will grow to be strong and blessed with a life filled with joy.

This method of divination gets its name from the Latin word *amnion*, which means a membrane.

ANTHROPOMANCY   An ancient and gruesome form of divination by means of interpreting the intestines of sacrificed children and women, much in the same fashion as haruspicy (divination by inspecting the entrails of slaughtered or sacrificed animals).

This horrible method of divination was believed to have been practiced regularly by the Emperor Julian the Apostate, and was at one time encouraged by the oracle at Delphi. However, by the sixth century B.C., the custom of human sacrifice had become "rare and repellent to the conscience" in the Greek world and was eventually outlawed entirely.

APANTOMANCY   The art and practice of drawing omens from chance meetings with animals or birds. (The old superstition of the black cat bringing bad luck when it crosses a person's path is one example of apantomancy which has survived to the present day.)

In Yorkshire, England, nineteenth-century fishermen were convinced that if a four-legged animal (especially a dog) happened to cross their paths while they were on the way to their boats in the harbor, it was an ominous portent. So great was their fear that many believed the only way to avert the pending misfortune was to kill the animal harbinger.

Meeting a rabbit or hare, according to the sixteenth century *Gospelles of Dystaues*, was an "evyll sygne." By the nineteenth century, a magickal method of protection against the bad omen of the hare was devised. It consisted of spitting over the left shoulder and then reciting the following charm:

"Hare before, trouble behind.
Change ye, Cross, and free me."

It is said that if a hare crosses your path from right to left, it foretells a disastrous journey ahead. However, if it crosses from left to right, it means good luck will soon be coming your way.

In some parts of England it was once believed that if a weasel crossed your path, it was an omen of treachery. In order to avert it, you were supposed to drop a coin on the road at the precise spot where the weasel crossed. The logic behind this was to avert the bad luck by transferring it to whomever found the coin and was unlucky enough to pick it up.

Apantomancy has been practiced throughout the world, probably since prehistoric times. Nearly all animals known to man have been connected with the arts of divination, but it seems that in Europe, Great Britain, and the United States of

America, cats, dogs, hares, bats, birds, and farm animals are the
types of animals interpreted more often than others.

ARITHMANCY (also known as arithmomancy)   The art and
practice of divination by interpretation of numbers and letter
values. It was practiced mainly by the ancient Greeks and
Chaldeans, and is the forerunner of numerology.

Arithmancy (which takes its name from the Greek words
arithmos meaning numbers, and *mancy*, which means divination,
was devised in Athens by the sixth-century philosopher
Pythagoras, who used it for character analysis as well as forecasting the future and fate of others.

ARITHMOMANCY (see ARITHMANCY)

ARMOMANCY (also known as scapulomancy)   The art and
practice of divination by observation of the shoulder bone of an
animal, usually one that has been properly sacrificed.

In China, it was a common practice among ancient diviners
to apply heat to the symbol-inscribed shoulder bone of an ox
until cracks forming various patterns appeared. These patterns
would then be interpreted.

(In addition to ox bones, Chinese diviners also were known
to use the carapace, or shell, of a tortoise in the same manner.)

As oxen were quite expensive, only those knowledge seek-
ers possessing great wealth could afford to have their futures divined by means of armomancy.

Divination by the shoulder bone of animals was also popular in ancient times among the Mohammedan diviners.

ART OF THE LITTLE DOTS   A relatively modern form of geomancy. It is quite simple and is performed in the following
way: If you are right-handed, hold a pen or pencil in your left

hand (or vice versa for lefties) over a blank piece of paper. Close
your eyes, clear your mind of all distracting thoughts, and then
quickly tap the tip of the writing instrument on the paper one
hundred times. Open your eyes and look at the paper. You will
see that a pattern has been formed by the random dots. Focus
your eyes and mind on the dot pattern until you are able to interpret its meaning.

ASPIDOMANCY   The art and practice of divination by sitting
on a shield within a magick circle and falling into a trance while
reciting ancient occult formulas. Once the state of trance has been
entered, the diviner is then able to experience divinatory visions
and/or to communicate with various gods and spirits in order to
receive spiritual advice or insight into events yet to occur.

(New York Public Library)

Aspidomancy was a method of divination popular at one time among the shamanic diviners of many Native American Indian tribes.

ASTRAGALI   Special divinatory dice used by the augurs of ancient times. They were carved from the four-sided knuckle-bones of sheep and decorated with dots, much in the same way as modern dice, or other symbols possessing divinatory significance.

Astragali were popular fortune-telling tools among the ancient Greeks, Romans, and Egyptians.

ASTRAGALOMANCY (also spelled astraglomancy)   The art and practice of divination by dice.

In primitive times, small bones such as the vertebrae were inscribed with special divinatory symbols and used by diviners to give answers to questions. In ancient Rome, Greece, and Egypt, the four-sided knucklebones of sheep were employed. (See ASTRAGALI)

Modern dice, as we know them, were believed to have been first used by the Egyptians around 1400 B.C.

To divine by dice is a fairly simple procedure. First, a list of twenty possible answers numbered from four to twenty-four must be written out. A question is asked out loud, and then a pair of ordinary dice are thrown. Their numbers are added together and written down. The dice are then thrown a second time, and their numbers are added to the first. The resulting number is then matched to the corresponding answer on the numbered list.

According to ancient occult tradition, Fridays and Sundays are the two most unfavorable days for the casting of the dice.

ASTRAGLOMANCY (See ASTRAGALOMANCY)

ASTRAGYROMANCY   Another form of astragalomancy or divination by dice. Three dice are cast into a circle about twelve inches in diameter. (If any or all of the dice fall out of the circle during the first two tries, the time for dice casting is said to be inauspicious, and you should not try again until a later time. Three misses in a row is considered an extremely unlucky sign.) The total face value of the dice is interpreted in the following manner:

Three is an indication of good luck. You may soon be receiving some unexpected good news.

Four is an indication of disappointment or a streak of bad luck. This is a time for you to be extremely careful.

Five means that your wish will be granted. A new friendship will soon be established.

Six is an indication that you will soon part with your money. Also, beware of dishonest friends.

Seven is an indication of sorrow and also setbacks. People are talking behind your back.

Eight is an indication that you will soon receive the blame for something which you may or may not be responsible for.

Nine is an indication of a wedding (either yours or someone close to you), luck in love, or a reconciliation of some kind.

Ten is an indication of a career advancement, or the birth of a child.

Eleven is an indication of sickness, a separation, sorrow for you or a loved one.

Twelve is an indication that you will be the recipient of happy news, either by phone or by mail.

Thirteen is a very bad omen, indicating sorrow, grief, and worry.

Fourteen is an indication that there is a secret admirer or a helpful friend.

Fifteen is an indication of disagreements, dishonesty, and gossip.

Sixteen is an indication of travel in store for you in the near future.

Seventeen is an indication that changes will soon be occurring. A possible change of residence within a year's time.

Eighteen is a very good omen, indicating success in all ventures, money, and happiness.

Another method of astragyromancy employs a circle divided into a dozen equal, pie-shaped wedges, each assigned a different letter of the alphabet from *A* to *L*. Three dice are cast into the circle, and the letters that are landed on are then interpreted using a prepared list of corresponding messages.

ASTRO-DIVINATION   The ancient occult science of casting astrological charts to answer specific, personal questions and/or to solve problems based on the position of the heavenly bodies at the time of the inquiry.

Also known by the name of Horary astrology, this form of astrological divination dates back to the fifth century B.C. (The word horary is derived from the Latin word *hora*, meaning hour.)

ASTROLOGY (also known as the science of the stars.)   An ancient occult art and science, dating back to the third century B.C. that judges the influence of the planets in the solar system on the course of human affairs.

In astrology, a planet's influence varies according to which section of the zodiac it is in.

The two main types of astrology are Mundane and Horary. Mundane astrology, which is based on the premise that the Earth's physical structure is affected by cosmic influences, deals with the prediction of large-scale phenomena such as earth-quakes, political trends, and wars. Horary astrology is a method that uses charts for answering specific questions and/or for solving problems.

The other branches of astrology include: Electorial astrology, which calculates appropriate dates and times for undertaking important events such as marriage, travel, and so forth; Inceptional astrology, which deals with the outcome of a particular event whose date, time, and place have already been established; Medical astrology, which correlates zodiac signs and planetary influences with diseases and malfunctions of the bodily organs; Natal astrology, which focuses on the horoscope of the heavens for the precise moment of an individual's birth; Pre-

Ancient Arab astrologers charting the position of the stars and planets to work out their predictions.
(Macrobius, *In Somnium Scipionis*, 1513)

dictive astrology, which predicts future events in an individual's life; and Astrometeorology, which uses the science of the stars to forecast weather patterns and conditions.

The twelve astrological signs of the zodiac and their attributes are as follows:

ARIES   (March 21–April 20)
   Symbol: The Ram
   Element: Fire
   Masculine/Positive
   Planetary Rulers: Mars and Pluto
   Gemstones: Coral and diamond
   Most compatible with: Aries, Leo, Sagittarius, and those with
      Moon in Aries.

TAURUS   (April 21–May 21)
   Symbol: The Bull
   Element: Earth
   Feminine/Negative
   Planetary Ruler: Venus
   Gemstones: Carnelian and emerald
   Most compatible with: Taurus, Virgo, Capricorn, and those
      with Moon in Taurus.

GEMINI   (May 22–June 21)
   Symbol: The Twins
   Element: Air
   Masculine/Positive
   Planetary Ruler: Mercury
   Gemstones: Agate and alexandrite
   Most compatible with: Gemini, Libra, Aquarius, and those
      with Moon in Gemini.

CANCER   (June 22–July 23)
  Symbol: The Crab
  Element: Water
  Feminine/Negative
  Planetary Ruler: The Moon
  Gemstones: Moonstone, pearl, and all white gemstones
  Most compatible with: Cancer, Scorpio, Pisces, and those
    with Moon in Cancer.

LEO   (July 24–August 23)
  Symbol: The Lion
  Element: Fire
  Masculine/Positive
  Planetary Ruler: The Sun
  Gemstones: Amber, ruby, and all yellow or golden-colored
    gemstones.
  Most compatible with: Leo, Sagittarius, Aries, and those with
    Moon in Leo.

VIRGO   (August 24–September 23)
  Symbol: The Virgin
  Element: Earth
  Feminine/Negative
  Planetary Ruler: Mercury
  Gemstones: Sapphire and sardonyx
  Most compatible with: Virgo, Capricorn, Taurus, and those
    with Moon in Virgo.

LIBRA   (September 24–October 23)
  Symbol: The Scales
  Element: Air
  Masculine/Positive

Planetary Ruler: Venus
Gemstones: Opal and tourmaline
Most compatible with: Libra, Aquarius, Gemini, and those
   with Moon in Libra.

SCORPIO   (October 24–November 22)
   Symbol: The Scorpion
   Element: Water
   Feminine/Negative
   Planetary Rulers: Mars and Pluto
   Gemstone: Topaz
   Most compatible with: Scorpio, Pisces, Cancer, and those
      with Moon in Scorpio.

SAGITTARIUS   (November 23–December 21)
   Symbol: The Centaur—Archer
   Element: Fire
   Masculine/Positive
   Planetary Ruler: Jupiter
   Gemstones: Turquoise and zircon
   Most compatible with: Sagittarius, Aries, Leo, and those with
      Moon in Sagittarius.

CAPRICORN   (December 22–January 19)
   Symbol: The Goat (or Goat-Fish)
   Element: Earth
   Feminine/Negative
   Planetary Ruler: Saturn
   Gemstones: Garnet, lapis lazuli, and all black gemstones
   Most compatible with: Capricorn, Taurus, Virgo, and those
      with Moon in Capricorn.

AQUARIUS   (January 20–February 19)
  Symbol: The Water-Bearer
  Element: Air
  Masculine/Positive
  Planetary Ruler: Uranus
  Gemstones: Amethyst and jacinth
  Most compatible with: Aquarius, Gemini, Libra, and those
    with Moon in Aquarius.

PISCES   (February 20–March 20)
  Symbol: The Fishes
  Element: Water
  Feminine/Negative
  Planetary Rulers: Jupiter and Neptune
  Gemstones: Aquamarine and bloodstone
  Most compatible with: Pisces, Cancer, Scorpio, and those
    with Moon in Pisces.

In astrology, the concept that different parts of the human anatomy are ruled by the twelve signs of the zodiac is known by the name zodiacal man. The divisions of control are: Aries rules the head and brain; Taurus rules the throat and neck; Gemini rules the shoulders, arms, and lungs; Cancer rules the chest and stomach; Leo rules the upper back, spine, and heart; Virgo rules the intestines and nervous system; Libra rules the lower back and kidneys; Scorpio rules the sex organs; Sagittarius rules the liver, thighs, and hips; Capricorn rules the knees, bones, teeth, and skin; Aquarius rules the calves, ankles, and blood; and Pisces rules the feet and lymph glands.

For more information, see Further Reading.

Sixteenth-century woodcut depicting astrology and the signs of the Zodiac, by Erhard Schon, Nuremburg

ASTROMANCY   The ancient name used for astrology; the art and practice of star-divination. It stems from the Greek word *astron* (meaning star), and was used mainly to describe the branch of astrology we now refer to as predictive astrology, which uses the stars to predict future events in a person's life. The term has lost its currency in modern times.

For more information, see ASTROLOGY, ASTRO-DIVINATION and HOROSCOPE.

ASTROMETEOROLOGY (see ASTROLOGY)

AUGURY has two definitions: (1) The art and practice of divination by the flight patterns or songs of birds.

Augury was a common practice in ancient Rome where appointed religious officials known as augurs foretold future events by observing and interpreting the many bird omens, which ranged from the type of bird seen to the direction of its flight, and so forth.

The ancient Romans also applied the term augury to divination by eclipses, as well as to thunder and lightning (which was believed to be a direct communication from the god Jupiter).

(2) The art, ability, or practice of the divinatory sciences in general.

See also ALECTRYOMANCY and ORNITHOMANCY.

AURAMANCY   The art and practice of divination by the aura (human or animal). This is a popular practice among many modern day Witches and Wiccans.

The aura is a colored light produced by heat and electromagnetic energy that emanates from the bodies of all living things; a psychic field of energy surrounding both animate and inanimate bodies. Except to those who possess psychic sensitivity, the aura is normally invisible to the naked eye.

There are two ways to perceive the aura. The first is, of course, by being born with the gift of aura vision as a natural ability. This talent usually runs in families and is passed down from generation to generation, sometimes skipping every other one. It often becomes apparent in early childhood; however there are certain cases where persons have discovered later in life that they have the gift.

There are also certain individuals who, through certain psychic exercises, can become adept at reading auras. However, in most of these cases there is evidence to suggest that clairvoyant tendencies were in place to begin with and merely needed to be cultivated.

The second way to perceive the aura is through a controversial technique known as Kirlian photography. Developed in the early 1940s by a Russian electrician and inventor named Semyon Davidovich Kirlian, this process captures glowing, multicolored emanations on film that are believed by many to be auras or biofields.

Kirlian photography is based upon the principle of the corona discharge phenomenon, and over the years many different Kirlian techniques have been invented.

In auramancy, the diviner seeks divinatory information in the colors and fluxes of the aura. For instance, according to Daniel Logan's *The Anatomy of Prophecy*, a white or light gold-colored aura indicates a spiritual and highly evolved soul that has lived many lifetimes and is now in its final incarnation on this plane of existence.

A yellow aura indicates a strong imagination and/or affirmative answers to specific problems facing the person. However, yellow combined with red (or an orange-colored aura) indicates confusion and a constantly changing nature. Red by itself is believed by some to be a negative aura color, indicating a person's deteriorating health or the presence of disease. The brighter the shade of red in an aura, the greater the likelihood of serious health problems. However, a red aura is considered by others to indicate a person with an outgoing nature.

Gray is perhaps the worst aura color for it is said to be an indication that the person will probably not live for very long. Gray auras are often seen emanating from persons who are in the final stages of a terminal illness, or those who are destined to soon die by accident, suicide, or at the hands of another.

Good health and/or the overcoming of personal karmic patterns from previous incarnations is indicated by an aura of blue, green, or a combination of the two colors. Blue also reveals a nurturing spirit, and green a person who likes to be around others.

Brown auras are usually seen around those who are dependable and who have a down to Earth nature.

When the color purple is present in an aura, it indicates that a material and/or spiritual healing is taking place. If a person's aura is a light shade of purple or lavender, it indicates that he or she possesses the natural ability to heal others. (This ability may or may not be known to the person at the time of the reading.) Violet is usually indicative of creative abilities.

Finally, an aura that appears black is said by some to actually be a combination of many colors which must first be sorted out before an accurate reading can be made. Other interpretations of the black aura include the presence of evil or demonic possession, an individual who carries around a curse, and a person possessing a rebellious nature.

In addition to the above-mentioned colors, images (either actual or symbolic) sometimes appear in the aura, which may be perceived by means of clairvoyance.

AUSTROMANCY   The ancient art and practice of drawing omens from the winds, and at one time, it was a popular belief that a bout of windy weather always presaged the hanging of a criminal.

The moaning of the wind outside of one's window is supposed to be an ill omen, usually an indication of a death taking place in the family. There is no doubt that this old superstition stems from the banshee of Gaelic folklore (a female nature spirit who sometimes takes the form of an old woman and who presages a death in the family by wailing a mournful tune that sounds like the melancholy moaning of the wind. As a herald of death, the banshee is usually heard at night under the window of the person who is about to die.)

In the practice of wind divination (which has probably been around since man first appeared on Earth), the speed, direction, and sound of the wind are the three main factors used for determining a divinatory message. Certain objects that are observed blowing in the wind are also significant.

In ancient times, diviners from China and Tibet practiced a form of austromancy which involved placing the open end of a seashell against the ear, and then drawing omens from the sounds heard within the shell.

AXINOMANCY (see AXIOMANCY.)

AXIOMANCY, (also known as axinomancy)   The art and practice of divination by an axe or hatchet. It is a method of divination that has been in practice since ancient times.

Properly interpreted, the quivering of the axe handle, when
driven into a post, is said to reveal the answers to questions. The
way the axe handle falls to the ground is an old method used
by diviners to point out the direction taken by a thief.

The axe has also been used as a tool to locate the exact spot
where treasure has been buried. Place a round agate on the
glowing edge of an axe that has been placed for some time in a
fire, taken out, and stood upright on the ground. If the gemstone sticks to the axe, it means that there is no treasure buried
under that spot. However, if the agate falls to the ground and
rolls around thrice in the same direction, it is an indication that
the treasure is buried below.

B

BELOMANCY   The art and practice of divination by arrows. It was extensively practiced among the Chaldeans, Babylonians, Scythians, and Arabs.

Three divining arrows marked with certain occult symbols, names, or prophetic inscriptions would be cast into a quiver, mixed together, and then one would be drawn and interpreted. In certain countries, wands or small wooden sticks were used instead of arrows. (See RHABDOMANCY.)

In the Bible, belomancy was practiced by Nebuchadrezzar (Ezek. xxi 21): "When he stood in the parting of the way . . . to use divination: he made his arrows bright."

BIBLIOMANCY (also known as stichomancy)   The art and practice of divination by means of opening a book at random and then interpreting in a prophetic fashion the first words or sentences read.

Just about any book can be used in the art of divination; however, grimoires and collections of poetry or prose appear to be the most popular among modern book-divining Witches.

Lots of the Saints is a Christianized form of bibliomancy, which employs the Gospels and the Holy Bible. For an answer to a specific question, or to receive symbolic messages regarding future events, open a Bible to a randomly selected page while your eyes are closed. Place the index finger of your right hand anywhere on the page, and then open your eyes. Whatever word or line your finger is pointing to can then be interpreted. (See LOTS OF THE SAINTS.)

Homeric Lots and Virgilian Lots are two ancient forms of bibliomancy involving randomly selected passages from the written works of Homer and Virgil, respectively, which are then interpreted to reveal future events or to answer a specific personal question. (See HOMERIC LOTS and VIRGILIAN LOTS.)

BLETONISM (See HYDROMANTIA.)

BOOK OF CHANGES (See I CHING.)

BOTANOMANCY The art and practice of divination by herbs or by burning branches of brier and vervain on which are inscribed specific questions to be answered. [Vervain is a plant which has long been associated with Witches, sorcerers, and the magickal arts, probably since the beginning of written history.]

The practice of botanomancy, which derives its name from the Greek word *botane* (meaning "herb"), can be traced back to the ancient Druid priests who believed in and worshipped the spirits of trees, particularly the oak.

The ancient Romans were also known to practice botanomancy, and their plant of choice was the laurel. They believed that by burning its leaves and then studying the ashes and/or smoke generated by it they could draw omens that would offer them guidance, warning, or a revelation of future events.

A number of references to botanomancy appear in the Old Testament. In the Second Book of Samuel (5:23–24) it is said that through the rustling of trees, David received holy information about the battle with the Philistines.

In modern times, botanomancy continues to be practiced in various ways. Two of its most simplest forms are the picking of a four-leaf clover and the blowing of seeds off the stalk of a dandelion and then making a wish.

Other methods of divination that are related to botanomancy are capnomancy, causimomancy, critomancy, cromniomancy, daphnomancy, phyllomancy, and phyllorhodomancy.

BRIZOMANCY   The art and practice of divination based on the prophetic inspiration of Brizo, an ancient goddess long worshiped in Delos. She delivered oracles in dreams to men and women who consulted her regarding seafaring and the business of fishing.

In order to receive her divine protection for those engaged on the sea, the women of Delos would present her with offerings consisting of miniature boats containing various types of food, except fish.

BUMPOLOGY   A nickname used by some for the art and practice of divination known as phrenology. (For more information, see PHRENOLOGY.)

C

CANCELLATION   A simple and traditionally youthful method of love divination whereby a young lady crosses out letters in the name of her beloved that match those in her own, and then uses the popular formula of "he loves me, he loves me not" to the remaining letters to find out whether or not the gentleman feels the same way about her.

(See LOVE DIVINATION.)

CAPNOMANCY   Is the ancient art and practice of reading portents from smoke rising up from a fire and by the way it drifts into the wind.

This method is often associated with sacrificial offerings to Pagan gods and flammable botanical material (such as poppy seeds, laurel leaves, or granulated incense) placed on hot coals or cast into a fire.

The practice of capnomancy is believed to have originated with the ancient Babylonians. On certain sacred days they would burn cedar branches or shavings, and then draw omens from the patterns of the smoke.

The Druids were also skilled in the art of capnomancy; however, they preferred reading the smoke generated by the burning of humans and animals on a sacrificial altar (a practice which earned them an infamous reputation and no doubt struck fear into the hearts of their enemies.)

A good omen was portended if the smoke rose straight up to the heavens. However, if it hung close to the sacrificial altar or touched the ground, this was taken as a warning that plans should be changed.

In the New England region of the northeast United States, weather conditions are forecast through a form of capnomancy by many folks who continue to practice the old ways of folklore.

According to this method, stormy weather or a bad omen of some sort is portended by chimney smoke that clings to the roof of a house, drifts to the ground, or pushes back down the chimney. When chimney smoke rises straight up to the sky, this is believed to indicate fair weather for both those who farm the land and sail the sea.

CARROMANCY (See CEROMANCY.)

CARTOMANCY   The art and practice of divination by means of interpreting cards—either regular playing cards, fortune-telling cards, or Zenner cards (a special pack of cards used in experimental tests for extrasensory perception, consisting of twenty-five cards, five of each of the following symbols: circle, cross, square, star, and a pattern of three wavy lines).

The practice of cartomancy is ancient and associated with Gypsy fortune-tellers. It is used to divine the future, as well as the past and the present.

The reading of Tarot cards (also known as tarotology) is the most popular method of card divination among most modern day Witches, New Agers, and students of the divinatory arts. (For more information, see TAROT.)

CATOPTROMANCY (also known as catoxtromancy)   The art and practice of divination by means of a special lens or magic mirror; an early form of scrying practiced by the ancient Greeks,

Old German Cards: Seven of clubs (*left*) and seven of spades. (New York Public Library)

using a mirror held in a fountain or turned to the light of the moon to catch lunar rays.

In ancient Rome, special diviners known as "blindfolded boys" were known to gaze into mirrors in order to experience visions of the future or of the unknown.

According to *Scriptores Historiae Augustae* of the fourth century A.D., the death of Julian the Apostate was accurately predicted by catoptromancers who had seen the emperor's death in a looking glass.

CATOXTROMANCY (See CATOPTROMANCY.)

CATTABOMANCY   The art and practice of divination by vessels made of brass, a metal believed to possess the supernatural power to repel evil spirits.

A nineteenth-century engraving depicting Michel de Nostradamus using his divinatory powers to make the royal destinies of the Queen's sons appear before her in a mirror. (Ann Ronan Picture Library)

Perfumed water, oil, ink, or some other liquid is poured into the vessel, and after special prayers and incantations are recited, the diviner gazes into the liquid without blinking, until he or she enters a trancelike state and is able to experience prophetic visions.

A related method is to place a brass plate upon a consecrated altar at midnight, while stating the information you desire to know. At dawn, according to legend, the answer will be written in dew upon the brass plate.

CAUSIMOMANCY   The art and practice of divination by observing special objects placed in a fire. When such an object

Many diviners believe that omens can be drawn
from how fast or how slow an object placed in a fire
burns. (Dover Publications)

cast into a fire smoldered and burned slowly or did not burn at
all, the omen connected to it was considered to be an unfavorable one. If the object burned rapidly, this indicted a favorable
omen.

This method of divination derives its name from the Greek
word *kaustos*, which means burned, and is a prognostication form
of capnomancy.

CELTIC CROSS (also known as the ten-card spread)   The traditional and most popular method of reading the cards of a
Tarot deck.

It is performed in the following manner: After the Tarot
cards have been thoroughly shuffled and cut three times, the
first card is turned up and placed in the number one position
(see diagram). This card represents the influences that are af-
fecting the querant (the person whose reading is being done)
along with his or her current situation.

In some instances, a Significator card (usually one of the Tarot court cards: King, Queen, Knight, Page) is laid down in the number one position of the diagram before the actual reading commences, and *then* the first card is picked from the shuffled deck and placed directly over the Significator in the same position to "cover him (or her)".

The second card is turned up and laid across the first one. This card "crosses him" (or her) and represents his or her obstacles.

The third card is turned up and placed above the Significator. This card "crowns him" (or her) and represents his or her future goals.

The fourth card is turned up and placed below the Significator. It is "what is beneath him" (or her) and represents the past.

The fifth card is turned up and placed to the right of the Significator. It is "what is behind him" (or her) and represents what is now passing away from him (or her), the more recent past.

The sixth card is turned up and placed to the left of the Significator. This card is "what is before him" (or her) and represents the immediate future, what is to come.

If done correctly, these six cards (plus the Significator) should form a cross with the Significator card located in the middle.

The next four cards (representing, in order, the man or woman whose reading is being done; his or her house/changes in environment; his or her hopes, fears and concerns; and the final outcome of the reading) are turned up on the right-hand side of the six-card cross in succession and positioned in a line, one above the other. (See the diagram on next page.)

CELTIC TREE ORACLE (See OGHAMIC DIVINATION.)

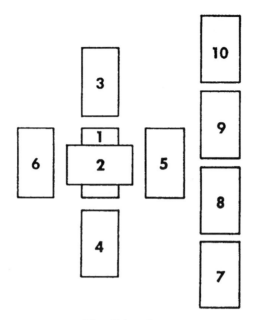

The Celtic Cross

CEPHALOMANCY (also known as kephalonomancy)   The art and practice of divination among the Lombards in which lighted carbon was poured on the baked head or skull of an ass or goat as the names of suspected criminals were called out. If a crackling occurred, it was believed that the man or woman whose name had been called out was guilty as charged.

CERAUNOSCOPY   The art and practice of divination by the interpretation of thunder and lightning, which at one time was believed to be a sign from or a direct communication with the gods, the Great Spirits, elementals, or other mystical entities.

In ancient Rome, augurs divined lightning in the following manner: Bolts from the East were favorable omens. Bolts from the West were considered to be unlucky. Bolts from the North were the most ominous of all, and bolts from the Northwest indicated that extremely bad news would soon be arriving.

Thunder "on the left" is lucky. Thunder "on the right" brings
a happy ending.

In the Middle Ages, it was believed that thunder and lightning in winter was a portent of war, summertime floods, or the
death of an important person living within a twenty-mile radius.

Thunder occurring on different days of the week portended
the deaths of certain types of people: Thunder on Sundays indicated the death of a learned man, a judge, or a general; on
Mondays it indicated the death of a woman; on Wednesdays the
death of harlots, and of other bloodshed; on Fridays the murder
of a great man; and on Saturdays it indicated widespread death
from the plague.

Thunder on Tuesdays was a good sign, indicating plenty of
grain. Thunder on Thursdays was also a favorable omen, meaning plenty of corn and sheep.

CEROMANCY (similar to molybdomancy, divination by molten lead poured into cold water)   The art and practice of divination by the melting of wax to form symbolic patterns.

Warm, melted wax is poured into cold water, and the seer
then interprets the shapes that are formed, such as significant
letters of the alphabet, numbers, or symbolic patterns.

Also known as ceroscopy and carromancy, this form of divination was developed by the ancient Romans and common at
one time in the countries of Britain, Sweden, and Lithuania.

In modern times it remains a popular practice among practitioners of divination throughout Puerto Rico and Mexico, and
also in certain parts of Haiti, where it is used in the sacred rites
of the Voodoo religion.

To divine using ceromancy, you will need a red candle, a shallow dish filled with water, a little bit of imagination, and an enormous amount of patience!

Light the candle and then meditate for one whole hour, focusing all of your thoughts and feelings on whatever it is that you seek to know. When the time is ready, hold the candle about eight inches over the plate and then slowly pour the melted wax onto the surface of the water. The wax will form a pattern of some sort and then instantly congeal.

Study the shape produced and then use your power of imagination to interpret the answer or message that the red wax holds for you. Always be on the lookout for letters of the alphabet, astrological symbols, and numbers for they are always highly significant.

CEROSCOPY (See CEROMANCY.)

CHALCOMANCY   The art and practice of divination by interpreting the tones produced by striking brass or copper chalices with special mallets.

It takes its name from the Latin *calix*, meaning communion-cup, and was a popular Tibetan method of divining the past, present, and future.

CHARACTEROLOGY (See SOMATOMANCY.)

CHARTOMANCY   The art and practice of divination by means of interpreting the writings in literary or musical works, official papers, and so forth.

This method takes its name from the Latin *charta*, meaning a paper, and is a form of bibliomancy (divination by books).

CHEIRO (See PALMIST.)

CHEIROGNOMY (also spelled chirognomy)   The study of the shapes of hands and fingers and what they reveal about a man's or woman's personality and physical health. It is a form of palmistry. (See PALMISTRY and CHEIROMANCY.)

CHEIROMANCY (also spelled chiromancy)   The art and practice of palmistry or palm reading; the study of the lines of the palm to disclose an individual's past and to predict their future.

There are seven important lines on the palm of the hand and seven lesser ones. The important or main ones are: The line of Life, the line of Head, the line of Heart, the girdle of Venus, the line of Health, the line of the Sun, and the line of Destiny. The seven lesser ones are: The line of Mars, the Via Lasciva, the line of Intuition, the line of Marriage, and the three bracelet lines on the wrist.

For more information, see PALMISTRY.

CHRESMOMANCY   The art and practice of divination by the utterances of a man or woman in a frenzy.

At the temple of Apollo in Delphi (the site of the most celebrated of Greek oracles), a female prophet known as the Pythia was consulted every month on the seventh day (the date of Apollo's birth). While in a frenzied state of trance, believed by Herodotus to have been induced by natural gases escaping from between the rocks, she was known to prophesy. Her utterances were interpreted by special divinatory priests, and they usually dealt with religious affairs.

CLEIDOMANCY (a form of radiesthesia)   The art and practice of divination by means of an enchanted key suspended on a string or thin chain from the third finger of a young virgin.

As in other forms of dowsing, the pendulum (or in this instance, the key) indicates a yes or no response to a particular question by the direction in which it swings or rotates. When held over a circle inscribed with letters and numbers, or a Ouija board, the key pendulum can be used by diviners to spell out messages from the spirit world.

Cleidomancy is similar to the radiesthesia related method of dactylomancy (the art and practice of divination by a dangling ring).

For more information, see RADIESTHESIA and DACTY-LOMANCY.

CLEROMANCY   A form of lot-casting. It is similar in practice to the art of divination by dice (astragalomancy) but simply employs small stones or pebbles of different colors in order to draw omens and divine fate.

For more information, see ASTRAGALOMANCY, LOTS, LOT-CASTING, and SORTITION.

COSCINOMANCY   The art and practice of divination by means of a sieve, which is suspended by tongs or pincers and supported by the middle fingers of two assistants.

The man or woman who has been accused of a crime is seated before the sieve, as the diviner recites the following magickal conjuration:

"DIES, MIES,
JESCHET, BENEDOEFET,
DOWIMA, ENITEMAUS"

The accused person's name is then said out loud, and (according to legend) his or her guilt is indicated if the sieve begins to rotate the moment the name is said.

This method of guilt divination was popular throughout France during the Middle Ages.

CRITHOMANCY (See ALPHITOMANCY.)

CRITOMANCY (See ALPHITOMANCY.)

CROMNIOMANCY The art and practice of divination by interpreting omens drawn from onion sprouts. Certain names are placed on onions, which are then buried in the ground. The one that sprouts first gives the required indication.

Another example: If an unmarried woman wishes to find out who her future husband will be, she should take some raw onions, and upon each one carve or write a different man's name or initials. She should then place the onions near a fire, and the man whose name is on the onion that sprouts first will be the one.

In some parts of the world, it is a tradition for young, unmarried women to practice this simple, yet effective, method of love divination on the first day of December.

CRYSTALOMANCY The art and practice of divination by crystals. The two main methods are scrying a magic mirror or crystal ball (crystal gazing) and reading quartz crystals to divine the past, present, and future (a method popular among many modern diviners of the New Age).

It is believed that the use of crystals to predict events of the future began around the year 1000 B.C. It is by far one of the oldest forms of divination that have survived into the present day.

As with other methods of scrying, the diviner should enter into a meditative state prior to consulting the crystal. For best results, the scrying should always take place in a darkened room with moonlight (preferably the bright rays from a full moon), candlelight, or some other light source reflecting off the surface of the crystal.

It is quite common for a clear crystal to suddenly appear cloudy to the scryer while he or she gazes into it. With enough concentration and practice, the cloudy images will transform into clear visions which can then be interpreted.

In addition to scrying, many modern Witches and New Agers alike enjoy utilizing the power of crystals for meditation, healing (especially of the chakras), developing or increasing psychic talents, and pendulum dowsing.

For more information, see SCRYING.

CUBOMANCY   The art and practice of divination by thimbles.

In the Victorian era, it was believed by many persons who subscribed to superstitious thought that if a woman was given three thimbles, it was an omen that marriage would never be in her future.

CYCLOMANCY   The art and practice of divination by a turning wheel marked with symbols, such as letters, numbers, words, names, astrological signs, certain occult symbols, and so forth. The wheel is given a sharp spin, and whatever marking is indicated by its pointer when the wheel stops spinning is then used as the divinatory message.

Such a wheel is known as a wheel of fortune, and it's a "good bet" that the roulette wheel as we know it today may have evolved from the ancient prognostication method of cyclomancy.

CYLICOMANCY (a form of scrying)   The ancient art and practice of divination by making images appear in water.

In early times, this was a common practice among warriors in India. Before heading into battle, they would gaze into a vessel of water. If their reflections did not appear, it was taken as an omen that they would not return home alive.

In Tahiti, diviners used cylicomancy to reveal the identity of thieves. A hole would first be dug in the earthen floor of the victim's house and then filled with water. After prayers and special incantations were recited, the diviner would then gaze into the water until the image of the thief's face appeared on the surface.

A popular variation of cylicomancy involves a bowl of water to which a bit of oil is poured on top of, thus forming divinatory patterns. With a bit of scrying skill, a diviner can gaze at the patterns and be able to interpret their true meanings.

In the Old Testament (Genesis 44:5 and 15), the prophet Joseph was said to have utilized a silver cup filled with water and oil in a similar fashion to look into the future.

D

DACTYLOMANCY   Is the art and practice of divination by means of employing an instrument similar to a tripod to spell out messages on a special board inscribed with letters of the alphabet, numbers, and/or symbols.

The precursor of the modern day Ouija board, dactylomancy dates back to the days of ancient Greece, and derives its name from the Phrygian sect of diviners and magicians known as the Dactyls, who practiced the mystic arts around 50 B.C.

DAPHNOMANCY   The art and practice of divination by interpreting the crackling of laurel branches thrown into an open fire. The louder the crackle, the more favorable the omen. However, if the branches are observed burning silently, this is taken as an evil sign.

The practice of daphnomancy originated in ancient Rome where there existed a sacred grove of laurel trees, made up of trees planted by each emperor when he ascended to the throne. It is interesting that in the year A.D. 68, the entire grove withered and died. This was taken as an extremely bad sign for the Roman Empire. That same year, the Emperor Nero died, and the long line of Caesars met its demise.

Daphnomancy takes its name from the nymph Daphne, who (according to Greek mythology) was magickally transformed into a laurel tree.

DEMONOMANCY The art and practice of divination through the evocation of demons.

In ancient Greece, demons were considered to be inferior divinities, such as deified heroes, and generally were thought to possess beneficial natures. (The word demon is derived from the Greek word *daimon*, meaning divine power, fate, or god. Many well-respected figures of early times, including the Greek philosopher Socrates, claimed to have been guided and protected by *daimons*.)

For many centuries, demons occupied a respected place as intermediary spirits between mortals and gods. But that all changed with the arrival of Christianity. Just as the Church transformed the old Pagan horned gods of fertility into their Devil, so did it turn all demons into hideous creatures of evil, unclean spirits, and agents of Satan.

Examples of demons, according to a sixteenth-century woodcut by Hans Holbein the Younger (from *Historiarum Veteris Testamenti icones*)

DENDROMANCY   The art and practice of divination by oak trees and mistletoes, a method common among the Druid priests of the ancient Celtic nations in Gaul, Britain, and Germany. They called it "divining the Golden Bough" and regarded it as a highly sacred rite.

According to sixteenth-century folklore, if an oak apple (a gall or swelling on an oak leaf caused by an insect known as a gallfly) is opened, and a worm is discovered within it, this indicates a life of poverty and strife. (A contradicting explanation is found in the *Athenian Oracle* which claims that a worm inside the oak apple is a prognostication of plenty.) If the worm should "run about," it presages the plague. If a spider is found, it is an omen of pestilence and scarcity of the corn crop. A fly presages war in the ensuing year.

A modern Witch's love divination calls for two acorns to be placed in a bucket filled with fresh rainwater. If they float toward each other and touch, it indicates true love and marriage; if they float away from each other, there will be no wedding in the near future.

The relatively modern custom of kissing under the mistletoe at Christmastime grew out of the ancient magickal and divinatory rites associated with this parasitic plant.

It was not at all unusual for a nineteenth-century maiden to sleep with a sprig of mistletoe under her pillow to induce a prophetic dream in which her future husband is revealed. This method was specially popular in Wales and England.

Another marriage divination involving mistletoe was to burn the previous year's mistletoe and interpret the flame. If it sputtered, it indicated a cruel or ill-tempered future husband. If it burned with a steady flame, it indicated a future husband who was loving, patient, and forgiving.

DIVINATION   The occult science, art, and practice of discovering the unknown, and foretelling events of the future by interpreting omens or by various methods of divination such as Tarot card reading, dice casting, gazing into crystal balls, consulting Ouija boards, using astrological calculations, and so forth.

Divination is a practice of the greatest antiquity. It has been performed in every culture in one style or another, and continues to be practiced in modern times (especially by astrologers, Witches, and Neo-Pagans).

There are two main classifications of divinatory methods: internal and external. The first is conditioned by change in the consciousness of the diviner. The second relies on sensory or mental impressions to reach a result.

Throughout the ages, persons who possessed the ability to divine have been known by many different names, including: augurs, soothsayers, seers, prophets, fortune-tellers, haruspices, scryers, stargazers, visionaries, dowsers, sign readers, and sibyls.

DIVINING ROD (See DOWSING.)

DOWSING   The art and practice of using a divining rod or pendulum to find subterranean water, hidden or buried treasure, missing persons, animals, or lost objects. According to legend, when the divining rod (which is a bent wire, or, more traditionally, a forked stick made of hazel, ash, rowan, or willow wood) is held over the source, it responds by either making quivering motions or bending downward.

Pendulum divination was given the name "radiesthesia" in the 1930s. Its name is derived from the Latin root for radiation and the Greek *aisthesis*, meaning feeling. (See RADIESTHESIA.)

Those who divine by dowsing are known as water-witches, water-wizards, or simply as dowsers.

One of the best-known dowsers of modern times is the Israeli psychic Uri Geller, who is said to be able to dowse with only his bare hands.

Dowsers locating precious metals with their divining rods. (From George Agricola, *De Re Metallica*, 1556.)

Dowsing is an ancient occult art said to be at least seven thousand years old. Its precise origins remain a mystery; however, it is known that dowsing was a method employed by the ancient Egyptians and Chinese kings.

DREAM DICTIONARIES Special books containing dream symbol interpretations. Some contain superstitions, and some contain a combination of the two.

One of the oldest formal writings on dream interpretation is *A Treatise of the Interpretation of Sundry Dreams*, which was originally published in the early seventeenth century. However, the oldest published dictionary of dreams and their occult significance is most likely the four-volume opus of dream interpretation written in the year A.D. 150 by the Greek soothsayer Artemidorus.

DREAM DIVINATION (See ONEIROMANCY.)

Œ

ELAEOMANCY (see HYDROMANTIA.)

EMPYROMANCY (see PYROMANCY.)

ENOPTROMANCY   The art and practice of divination by suspending a mirror over a bowl of water and then gazing into the mirror until visions of a divinatory nature appear on its surface.

A form of both hydromantia and scrying, this method of foretelling is common among many psychic healers who employ it to gain insight from the spirit world and/or the psychic realm relating to a patient's condition, recuperation, or death.

EPATOSCOMANCY   The art and practice of divination by examination of the viscera of human sacrifices, and a form of the divinatory art known as anthropomancy.

In ancient times it was regularly practiced and accepted as part of the formal religions of such cultures as the Babylonians, Greeks, Romans, Japanese, and Sumerians.

Epatoscomancy is frequently mentioned in the Bible. The Book of Ezekiel describes this gruesome method being carried out by the king of Babylon, and in the second book of Kings, King Ahaz of Judah is said to have practiced it as well.

In North America, the Comanche and other native tribes

were, at one time, also skilled in the art of epatoscomancy, as were the Incas and the Aztecs.

Civilized cultures no longer consider the sacrificing of humans (or animals) to be an acceptable method of divination; however, in certain remote regions of this world, this practice (or variations of it) no doubt is still very much alive.

E.S.P. (see EXTRASENSORY PERCEPTION.)

EXTISPICIOMANCY   Closely related to the art and practice of epatoscomancy, extispiciomancy draws omens from the viscera of sacrificed animals.

For more information, see ANTHROPOMANCY; EPATO-SCOMANCY; HEPATOMANCY.

EXTRASENSORY PERCEPTION (also known as E.S.P.)   The awareness of events not presented to any of the bodily faculties of perception or feeling.

Such metaphysical abilities as channeling, premonitory dreaming, psychometry, and telepathy are all regarded as different forms of extrasensory perception.

Most E.S.P. researchers agree that all persons possess psychic or extrasensory abilities to one degree or another. However, not all individuals are aware of their "gifts," and in many cases, certain people naturally possess stronger abilities than others. Whether these abilities are expressed or inhibited often depends greatly on a person's mental disposition, interest, and manner of action.

F

FELIDOMANCY   The art and practice of divination by the behavior and actions of cats.

Since early times, the mysterious cat has been associated with Witches and the occult arts, and many superstitious folks have looked upon them with both fear and fascination. Cats were said to possess magickal powers and psychic abilities. They were also believed to be the familiars of Witches. Some cats were actually shape-shifting Witches in disguise!

Possessing such a supernatural reputation, it is not surprising that the feline has long been used by diviners searching for clues to the future.

Using the behavior of a cat to predict the weather is perhaps the oldest and most common method of felidomancy. For instance: If a cat turns its tail to the fire, this foretells a change of weather, particularly rain or a hard frost. (It is also taken as an omen of ill luck.) Stormy weather is on its way if a cat lies curled up with its forehead touching the ground or if it is observed washing behind its ears. (Whichever direction the cat faces while it washes is said to be the direction from which the winds of the storm will blow.)

If a grooming cat puts its paw around its right ear, this is said to mean that a gentleman will soon come to visit; around the left ear means a lady. If a strange black cat suddenly enters your house, it is an omen of good fortune. (However, bad luck will befall you if you should try to chase it away or harm it in any manner.)

Felidomancy is a form of zoomancy (divination by observation of animal behavior); however, it should not be confused with the method known as apantomancy, which draws omens from chance meetings with animals or birds (a black cat crossing one's path, for example).

FIRE OF AZRAEL   The name given to a special fire used for the purpose of divining. (see FIRE SCRYING.)

FIRE SCRYING   The art and practice of divination by interpretation of symbolic visions of the past, present, and/or future received while scrying (gazing) into flames or burning embers. (Any fire used for this purpose is known as a "fire of Azrael.")

As with crystal scrying, fire scrying is an occult art that takes much practice and patience. It has been around probably since prehistoric times and has been practiced by diviners from all cultures.

Often, the visions seen while scrying a fire are symbolic in nature rather than actual. For instance: blue colored flames signify the presence of spirits; white flames indicate good luck or good health; the image of a coffin seen in the flames could indicate a funeral in the near future; a number appearing in the flames or embers could be a significant date, address, lottery number; and so forth.

Fire scrying is believed to be a form of psychic communication received in a state of trance that is attained through the prolonged gazing at the flames.

FLORAL ORACLE   A system of flower divination devised by Rinoir Montaire, a professor at the University of Lyons (France). It reached its height of popularity in the middle of the eigh-

An elemental spirit appears in a fire. (Michael Majer,
Scrutinium Chymicum, 1687)

teenth century, and was used to reveal a person's underlying
character and to divine their future career. This was done with
a large bouquet filled with various types of flowers. A person
would first make a careful study of the bouquet and then pick
the one flower that appealed to them over the rest. The reading would then be based upon the divinatory meaning of the
picked flower. (For instance: A lily indicated a promising career
in politics while an apple blossom revealed a career as a practi-
tioner of law.)

FLOROMANCY   The art and practice of divination by the observation of flowers or plants. (One of the most popular uses for
floromancy is for love divination.)

Divination by flowers was a popular method of
prophecy throughout Europe and the United States
during the Victorian era. (Dover Publications)

In Victorian England, two flowers that had not yet blos-
somed would be paired, and the initials of certain lovers' names
would be placed on the stems. These flowers would then be
placed in a secret place and observed by the diviner for ten con-
secutive days. If after that time any flower twined the other, it
indicated marriage for the man and woman whose initials were
used. A blossom indicated children (the number of children determined by the number of blossoms); the death of a flower indicated a breakup or the death of one of the lovers; and so forth.

Another popular method of floromancy was the Floral Oracle,
which is also covered in this chapter. (see FLORAL ORACLE.)

FORECAST   A psychic or astrological prediction concerning
future events. When used as a verb, this word means to predict
the future by means of astrology, dreams, or clairvoyant powers.

FORTUNE COOKIE (see ALEUROMANCY.)

FORTUNE-TELLER   A woman or man who is able to predict future events in a person's life through various forms of divination, such as palmistry, numerology, Tarot cards, and so forth; a diviner, augur, soothsayer, etc.

Most serious practitioners of modern divination prefer to call themselves diviners or practitioners of the occult sciences rather than fortune-tellers as the latter has the connotation of being a charlatan and is often used in a derogatory manner. (The mental images most commonly conjured up by the word fortune-teller are of carnival sideshows and unscrupulous con artists clad in gaudy Gypsy costumes.)

GASTROMANCY According to John Gaule's *Mysmantia* (1652), gastromancy is the art and practice of divination "by the sound of or signs upon the belly."

This peculiar method of drawing omens takes its name from the Greek word *gaster* (the stomach).

It is considered to be an ancient form of ventriloquism. The diviner, standing over a particular grave in a cemetery, would first enter a state of trance and then begin uttering prophecies with his voice lowered to a sepulchral tone, as though it was coming from the grave below.

GELOMANCY (See GELOSCOPY.)

GELOSCOPY The art and practice of divination by interpreting the sound of hysterical laughter, traditionally of a prophesying medium in a state of divinatory mania.

From this ancient method of gaining insight into the future, evolved the old superstitious belief that if you "laugh till you cry," you'll have "sorrow till you die."

GEMATRIA A cabalistic, cryptographic art and practice of divination by means of interpreting number and letter symbolism, significant in Jewish mysticism, and an early form of numerology.

Using any of several mathematical methods (often extremely complicated ones), special numerical values are assigned to the letters of words. Thus, any two words or sentences sharing the same number values were regarded as identical in meaning or truth, and could then be interchanged in order to divine a new meaning from any passage of the Hebrew Scriptures.

The practice of gematria dates back to the eighth century B.C., and it has been used, for example, by the ancient Greeks to divine dreams; by medieval Kabbalists to find the secret and powerful name of God; by diviners to interpret the Old Testament; and by Ceremonial Magicians to establish new words of power which were employed in conjuring and incantations.

GENETHLIALOGY   The astrological science, art, and practice of calculating future events and studying personal characteristics from the influence of the stars at the moment of a person's birth.

For more information, see ASTROLOGY, ASTRO-DIVINATION, HOROSCOPE, etc.

GEOMANCY   The art and practice of divination by means of casting pebbles on dirt or sand, connecting the points, and then interpreting the pattern formed.

Other methods of geomancy include random dots made with a pencil or pen on a sheet of paper (known as the "Art of the Little Dots"), the interpreting of shifting sand, and Chinese geomancy (which is known as *Feng Shui*).

Geomancy, which literally translates as earth divination, is probably as old as astrology, and is said to be the surviving ancestor of the *I Ching*. It originated in the country of Persia, (now known as Iran), and its practice was at one time widespread throughout the Mediterranean region, the near East, and Africa (where it was known as *fa* or *djabe*).

In the mid-sixteenth century, the first full description of geomancy appeared in Cornelius Agrippa's second book, *Occult Philosophy*.

GRAPHOLOGY   The art and practice of character analysis from handwriting; handwriting analysis.

In graphology, details of the breadth and height of each letter, the degree of slant, space between lines, letters and words, and general presentation are taken into consideration.

In the year 1622, the first treatise on the subject of handwriting analysis appeared, and, in the late nineteenth century, efforts at graphological systemization began with the work of the French abbe Hypolite Michon (1806–1881).

The science of graphology (which is often regarded as an occult science, although it is never used in a predictive capacity) is divided into two schools of thought: Gestalt and Trait-stroke. The Gestalt theory teaches that a complete personality picture is made by the movement, form, and arrangement of handwriting, and that these elements must be analyzed altogether. The Trait-stroke theory teaches that each individual stroke possesses a different meaning.

Theoretically, the page symbolizes the world, and the handwriting (which consists of over twenty elements) symbolizes the different, yet interrelated, aspects of the writer's personality and his or her relationship with the world.

Handwriting, which is a direct projection from the brain, is said to accurately reveal people's true feelings about themselves, what motivates them, how they react to any given situation, whether or not they are likely to realize their goals, and so on.

Many graphologists use a unique method of handwriting analysis which divides each letter of the alphabet into three parts (upper, middle, and lower) to reveal the writer's physical and sexual qualities, emotions, and spirituality.

GYROMANCY   An ancient method of divining the past, present, and future, taking its name from the Latin word *gyrare* (to turn or whirl); divination by rounds or circles.

It is performed in the following manner: A circle is drawn upon the ground when the Moon is positioned in the appropriate astrological position. Special prayers or incantations are recited, and then a person, or group of persons, enters the circle and begins walking in circles until they fall from dizziness and begin uttering predictions.

A similar version was to interpret the prophetic utterances of persons exhausted by frenzied dancing around an enchanted circle.

In yet another method of gyromancy, the circle is marked with special words, letters of the alphabet, numbers, runes, or symbols of an occult, astrological, or religious nature. Each time a person walking or dancing around the circle stumbled, the word or symbol marked at that point would be recorded by the diviner and used to spell out a prophecy.

ℏ

HALOMANCY (See ALOMANCY.)

HANDWRITING ANALYSIS (See GRAPHOLOGY.)

HARUSPEX   In ancient Rome, a special priest who was skilled in the divinatory art of haruspicy was known as a haruspex or aruspex. (Plural: haruspices.)

The duty of the divination priest was to interpret omens and draw predictions from the entrails of slaughtered or sacrificed animals and birds. His position was a well-respected one, and, like the augur, he was usually consulted by the emperor or other government officials before any major political or military move was made.

The main thing the haruspices observed was the liver and its pyramid-shaped projection known as the *processus pyramidalis*.

For more information, see HARUSPICY.

HARUSPICATION (See HARUSPICY.)

HARUSPICY (also known as haruspication)   The art and practice of divination by means of inspecting the entrails of slaughtered or sacrificed animals and birds.

Every year during the pre-Christian sun god festival known as *Inti Raymi* (which was always celebrated on the twenty-fourth day of June), in the country of Peru, llamas were ritually slaughtered, and their entrails were used by Incan priests for divining the future.

The barbarous practice of haruspicy was also common among the ancient Romans and Greeks, who most likely were introduced to it by the Etruscans or the earlier cultures of Babylonia and Assyria.

For more information, see HARUSPEX.

HELIOMANCY   The art and practice of divination by the sun, including solar eclipses.

Solar divination (which was under the domain of all gods and goddesses connected to the Sun) has been practiced since prehistoric times in all parts of the world, and is rooted in the

Ancient diviners using the intestines of a sacrificial goat to divine the future. (From a German edition of Petrarch's *De Remediis Utriusque Fortunae*, Douce Collection, Bodleian Library, Oxford, England.)

sun-worshipping cults of early man. The name of this particular form of divination is derived from *Helios*, the name of the Greek god of the Sun.

An eclipse of the Sun was at one time believed to be a serious omen of misfortune for both man and the Earth. Primitive man and woman must surely have been terrified by such a strange event in the sky above them.

The sudden appearance of the Sun during a rainstorm is deemed a lucky sign by many, while others read omens in the particular colors of sunsets.

Although it's true that its original purpose remains unknown today, it has been suggested that Stonehenge, the mysterious stone circle on the Salisbury Plain in Wiltshire, England, was at one time used as a sacred temple for sun divination by the ancient Druid priests.

HEMOMANCY   The ancient art and practice of divination by blood, usually of a sacrificed animal or human being. Blood sacrifices were common at one time in Africa, Asia, and among aboriginal Americans and Europeans in prehistoric times. In some cultures, the menstrual blood of virgins was used to divine fate.

Blood divination was usually performed by spilling fresh blood onto a special white cloth and then drawing omens from the various patterns which formed.

Among Christians, the religious phenomenon or miracle of stigmata (the spontaneous bleeding from invisible wounds resembling the five wounds of Jesus Christ) is taken as a divinatory sign from God. Stigmata have been associated with certain saints and deeply religious men, women, and children.

In early nineteenth-century Scotland, it was believed (especially among fishermen and their families) that to shed blood on the first day of the new year was a favorable omen indicating good fortune.

HEPATOSCOPY   The art and practice of divination by means of interpreting the liver of a sacrificed sheep; liver-gazing. This gruesome form of divination was a common practice among the ancient Romans, Babylonians, Etruscans, and Hittites.

The main thing observed by hepatoscopists was the liver's pyramid-shaped projection called the *processus pyramidalis*. A large one was considered to be a favorable omen; a cleft one indicated trouble; and a missing one was taken as the gravest omen of them all.

HERBS ASSOCIATED WITH DIVINATION   Acacia, adder's tongue, camphor, cloves, cowslip, daisy, dandelion, frankincense, goldenrod, hawthorn flowers, hibiscus, honeysuckle, lemon grass, mace, mugwort, nutmeg, orris root, peppermint, rose, thyme, vervain, wormwood, and yarrow.

HIEROMANCY (also known as hieroscopy)   The art and practice of divination by means of drawing prophetic conclusions from objects of ancient sacrifice.

This method takes its name from the Greek words *hieros*, meaning holy. It is closely related to the divinatory arts of haruspicy or haruspication (divination by the entrails of sacrificed animals), hepatoscopy (divination by the liver of sacrificed animals, especially sheep), and anthropomancy (divination by the intestines of sacrificed children and women).

See HARUSPICY, HEPATOSCOPY, and ANTHROPO-MANCY.

HIEROSCOPY (See HIEROMANCY.)

HIPPOMANCY   The art and practice of divination by interpreting the way a horse neighs or stamps its hooves, or by observing its gait during ceremonial processions.

A medieval woodcut showing a Witch and the Devil riding on the back of an enchanted horse. (From the Mansell Collection, London, 1493.)

Since early times, the horse has been used by many to divine illness, love, sorcery, and the fate of humans. It is considered to be one of the most psychic of all animals, and it is said to possess the supernatural ability to both see and communicate with the spirits of the dead.

HOMERIC LOTS   A form of bibliomancy (book divination) involving randomly selected passages from the written works of Homer, which are then interpreted in the hopes of revealing future events or gaining the answer to a specific, personal question.

This method of divination was first practiced in ancient Greece, where it was known as *sortes Homericae*, and the book most commonly employed was *The Iliad*.

In the distant past, it was not uncommon for diviners to look to the great poets for hidden clues to the future. The written works of Virgil were also used in a similar fashion. (See VIR-GILIAN LOTS for more information.)

HORARY ASTROLOGY One of the two main types of as-trology (the other is called Mundane). It is an ancient astrolog-ical method which employs special charts for answering questions and/or solving specific problems. It is named after the Latin *hora*, which means an hour.

For more information, see ASTROLOGY and also ASTRO-DIVINATION.

HOROSCOPE In astrology, it is a chart of the heavenly bod-ies that shows the relative positions of the planets at a certain moment in time.

Given the exact time and place of an individual's birth, an as-trologer can cast a horoscope from which he or she can define the subject's character and advise them on future courses of action.

For more information, see ASTROLOGY, ASTRO-DIVINA-TION, and HOROSCOPY.

HOROSCOPY The art and practice of divination by casting astrological horoscopes; also known as predictive astrology. It dates back to ancient times and is perhaps the most popular form of divination that has survived into the present day.

For more information, see ASTROLOGY, ASTRO-DIVINATION, and HOROSCOPE.

HYDATOSCOPY The art and practice of divination by ex-amination of rainwater. In this method, which is a form of hy-dromantia, omens are drawn from the various formations and sizes of rain puddles, and bowls of rainwater are gazed upon (see SCRYING) until clairvoyant visions appear on the surface of the water or in the mind's eye.

A sixteenth-century woodcut showing a woman
giving birth as two stargazers prepare the baby's
horoscope.

Hydatoscopy has been practiced since ancient times at all
levels of culture. (For more information, see HYDROMANCY
and HYDROMANTIA.)

HYDROMANCY   The art and practice of divination by water,
by things dropped into water, or by gazing (scrying) into water
surfaces.

The following methods are just a few examples of hydromancy: Predicting future events by interpreting rings formed on

the surface of a cup of water into which a gemstone, wedding ring, or amulet has been dropped; gazing into a pail of water to locate lost or stolen objects, or to see the face of a thief; drawing omens by observing all details of the water in a stream or river, such as the direction of its flow, its movement, and whether it is calm or restless.

Hydromancy has been practiced since ancient times in nearly every area of the world, but most commonly in New Guinea, Scandinavia, Tahiti, and the Hawaiian islands.

HYDROMANTIA   A hydromantic form of divination in which a seer or inquirer gazes fixedly into a silver cup or pool of still water to see the future or to make gods, demons, or spirits appear in the water.

Other forms of hydromantic divination include bletonism (divination by currents of water), elaeomancy (divination by observing a liquid surface), hydatoscopy (divination by rainwater), lecanomancy (divination by basins of water), and pegomancy (divination by bubbling fountains of water).

These methods are practically universal in antiquity and remain popular practices among many modern day diviners.

HYLOMANCY (See PSYCHOMETRY.)

I

I CHING (THE BOOK OF CHANGES)   The ancient Chinese science of synchronicity, dating back to the very beginning of Chinese civilization. It is based on a group of sixty-four six-line drawings called hexagrams that describe the patterns of change and transformation.

I Ching (pronounced ee-jing) teaches that the womb of the universe is a limited, imperceptible void—*T'ai Chi*, the Absolute. In it, everything has its being, and each owes its individuality to a particular combination of Yin (negative) and Yang (positive). See YIN AND YANG.

To consult the *I Ching* for advice or answers to questions, three coins are tossed, or a counting game with fifty yarrow sticks is played, in order to randomly produce one of the hexagrams. When properly interpreted, the hexagram reveals either fortune or misfortune, which can be used in divination and for personal consultation.

The *I Ching*, which is said to have originated in the country of China during the Bronze Age (sometime between 100 and 500 B.C.), is believed by many to open up the doorway to psychic insight, intuitive knowledge, and spiritual harmony. Unlike most other methods of fortune-telling, the *I Ching* suggests possibilities rather than making direct predictions. It also recommends a course of action, in addition to predicting the outcome of a series of events.

In the West, the *I Ching* *(Book of Changes)* was virtually unheard of until the year 1882 when it was translated into the English language by the British scholar James Legge.

ICHYOMANCY (See ICHTHYOMANCY.)

ICHTHYOMANCY   The art and practice of divination by the examination of fish, either living or dead, and especially by interpreting the entrails of fish. It should only be performed when the Moon is positioned in the astrological sign of Pisces (the Fish), according to occult tradition.

This form of divination takes its name from Ichthys, the son of the goddess Atargatis (Ashtart or Astarte), and it is connected to the ancient Asiatic rites which embraced the worship of the fish as a sacred creature. (Incidentally, the Greek word for fish happens to be *ichthus*.)

Fish divination was a popular practice among the ancient Assyrians, Babylonians, Chinese, and Phoenicians.

K

KEPHALONOMANCY (See CEPHALOMANCY.)

KUA   A system of sixty-four hexagrams used in the Chinese method of divination known as the *I Ching* or *Book of Changes*. Each hexagram consists of a block of six solid or broken horizontal lines each possessing a different meaning.

For more information, see *I CHING* (THE BOOK OF CHANGES) and also YIN AND YANG.

L

LAMPADOMANCY   The art and practice of divination based on the observation of the movement of a lamp's flame.

This method of divination was popular among diviners in ancient Egypt, who performed it at midday in a darkened room illuminated by a lamp filled with oasis oil. Magickal spells would be recited, and then a trancelike state would be entered, in which spirits or gods would be seen in or around the flame of the lamp. The diviner would then attempt to communicate with the spiritual entities in the hopes of obtaining divinatory knowledge and/or receiving advice on particular matters.

LECANOMANCY (a form of hydromantia)   The art and practice of divination by means of dropping small precious stones or other objects into basins of water. The resulting images and sounds would then be interpreted.

Also known as leconomancy, this method of prognostication is believed to have been developed by the ancient Assyrians. They would use a special bowl of water covered by a thin layer of oil obtained from the melted fat of an animal. After a question was asked, a consecrated pebble marked with religious/magickal symbols would be dropped into the bowl by a diviner-priest. Whether or not the oil separated determined the final prophecy.

For additional information, see HYDROMANCY and also HYDROMANTIA.

LIBANOMANCY (also known as libranomancy) The art and practice of divination by incense and observation of its smoke. A similar method, livanomancy, is concerned primarily with divination by the burning of frankincense.

Incense divination dates back to pre-Christian times. How slow or fast the incense burned, as well as the formations and directions taken by its smoke, all possessed divinatory significance in answering particular questions, identifying guilty parties, and so forth.

One form of libanomancy practiced by the Popoluca of Veracruz (Mexico) was carried out in the following fashion: Into a pot containing water were tossed small balls of copal incense. This was done as the diviner asked a question out loud, presumably to the gods. If the incense floated, it indicated a yes answer. However, if it sank to the bottom of the pot, it meant that the answer was no.

Incense was, and still is, an essential tool in the occult art of divination. In addition to its aforementioned usages, incense is beneficial for invoking the spirits which aid in divination or enable the diviner to meditate properly and enter a trance or shamanic state of consciousness. While in this state, he or she may witness divinatory visions or be able to communicate directly or symbolically with spirit entities, angelic beings, or deities.

LIBRANOMANCY (See LIBANOMANCY.)

LITHOMANCY The art and practice of divination by stones, an old method of fortune-telling which was at one time quite popular in Great Britain and throughout much of Europe.

Lithomancy is usually performed in one of two different ways: By casting thirteen smooth pebbles or crystals in lots, and then drawing omens from the position in which they land; or by interpreting the reflection of candlelight in precious stones or glass beads.

In the first method, the thirteen stones represent the Sun, the Moon, Mars, Venus, Mercury, Jupiter, Saturn, the home, love life, health matters, magick, fortune, and news.

In the second method, which is traditionally performed by arranging the stones or beads around a burning white candle, the color of the reflections are utilized in determining a divinatory message. For instance: A blue reflection signifies good luck, peace, tranquility, or a healing (either physically or spiritually); a black or gray one foretells misfortune, sickness, death, or the presence of evil; red indicates love, a sexual relationship, and/or marriage; yellow is said to mean betrayal; a purple reflection signifies sorrow in the near future; green is the sign of success in all ventures; and so forth.

Lithomancy takes its name from *lithos*, a Greek word meaning stone.

LIVANOMANCY (See LIBANOMANCY.)

LOGARITHMANCY   The art and practice of divination by logarithm (a method of reducing arithmetical calculations to a minimum by substituting addition and subtraction for multiplication and division).

This form of divination, which is related to numerology, takes its name from the Greek words *logos* (meaning ratio), and *arithmos* (a number).

LOT CASTING (also known as sortition)   The art and practice of foretelling future events or determining the answer to a previously thought-of question by the casting of lots (usually two objects, of which one is marked with the word yes and the other is marked with the word no) or some other chance choice.

The casting of lots is perhaps the oldest form of divination known to mankind, and its practice is described both in the works of Homer and in the Old Testament. (See URIM AND THUMMIN.)

Numerous methods of lot casting have been devised throughout the ages, and various objects, including dice, slips of paper, stones, knucklebones, and pieces of wood, have been used as lots. (See LOTS.)

LOTS   In the art and practice of lot casting or sortition, lots are any of various objects marked with special words, letters, numbers, colors, and/or symbols.

They are cast for the purpose of divining future events or for determining the answer to a previously thought-of question. (See LOT CASTING.)

The singular lot is a person's fate or destiny.

LOTS OF THE SAINTS   A Christianized form of bibliomancy (book divination) which uses the Gospels and the Bible. (See BIBLIOMANCY.)

For an answer to a particular question, or to receive symbolic messages regarding future events, the Bible is opened at a randomly selected page, and the first word or line read is then interpreted.

To discover the true identity of a thief or sorcerer, a key is placed in the Bible with the handle out. The key's handle is then held by a person who recites the following incantation:

> "Turn Bible, turn key.
> Turn and show the name to me."

A list of names is read off, and when the correct name is mentioned, the key is supposed to begin turning.

Another version of the Bible and Key method was to have a group of persons suspected of stealing gather around a table upon which a Holy Bible is placed. Upon the Bible is laid a key. The owner of the stolen property takes the key by the middle and gives it a fast spin. The person sitting opposite to whom the spinning key stops is identified as the guilty culprit.

This method of divination was practiced in Great Britain and throughout Europe during medieval times and the Reformation era. It remained popular in many rural communities of Great Britain well into the nineteenth century.

The Bible was also used by medieval maidens to divine the initials of their future husband's names. This was done by inserting a key in a Bible exactly over the sixth and seventh verses of the last chapter of Solomon's Song. The inquirer ties the Bible closely together with the garter from her right knee and then she and another young lady suspend it by both placing their middle fingers under the key's bow. Two verses are read for every letter of the alphabet or the following incantation is recited:

> "If the letter A [B,C,etc.] begins
> my true lover's name,
> may the Holy Bible turn
> and the key do the same."

When the correct initial is reached, the Bible will begin to turn around by itself.

To reveal if your lover has been unfaithful to you, place a key between the pages of the Book of Ruth. With another per-

Since medieval times, the Bible has been consulted by
diviners to identify thieves, sorcerers, future marriage
mates, and unfaithful lovers. (Sixteenth-century woodcut.)

son, balance the key by the bow with the middle finger of your right hands, and then repeat this magickal incantation:

"Many waters cannot quench true love,
neither can the floods drown it.
Love is as strong as Death
but jealousy is as cruel as the grave
and burneth with a most vehement flame.
If a man should give all the substance
of his house for love,
it would be utterly consumed."

If the Bible then turns to the right, it indicates that your lover has been faithful. However, if it turns to the left, he or she has been false and fickle.

LOVE DIVINATION   An occult practice of the greatest antiquity, and countless means have been used in the past, and are still used today, for this purpose.

Love divination is a form of sympathetic magick. Its practice (past and present) is universal, and it has always been a vital part of the Old Religion.

It was widely practiced by temple magicians of ancient Egypt, the augurs of Rome, Mexico, and Peru, and by many of the Native American Indian tribes of North America.

Many twentieth-century customs are rooted in the ancient practice of love divination. For instance, the relatively modern Halloween custom of bobbing for apples is actually a remnant of ancient Druidic divination rites.

Love divinations are traditionally performed by many modern Witches on Saint Valentine's Day (February 14th) and Saint

Fifteenth-century woodcut

Agnes' Eve (the night of January 20th when, according to folk legend, an unmarried woman will be able to catch a glimpse of her future husband or lover in a dream).
See also CANCELLATION and LOVE NUMEROLOGY.

LOVE NUMEROLOGY   A simple and modern method of numerology used by diviners to reveal whether or not a particular person will be their ideal love mate. This is done by using a basic numerology chart (see the one on the next page) to establish both persons' "love number." If both of these numbers match, a happy and lasting relationship is indicated. The further apart the numbers are from each other (for instance, one and nine), the greater the chances are that the relationship will not be a successful one.

    To find out what your "love number" is, simply add up the numerological values of your full name, first, middle, and last, (using the chart) with the date of your birth (as numerals, not spelled out). Add three (the mystical number of magick) and then add together the digits of the total number if higher than nine until the number is reduced to a single-digit number.

1	2	3	4	5	6	7	8	9
A	B	C	D	E	F	G	H	I
J	K	L	M	N	O	P	Q	R
S	T	U	V	W	X	Y	Z	

LYCHNOMANCY   The art and practice of divination by observing the flames of three candles arranged to form a triangle.

In the nature religion of Wicca, the triangle is a sacred symbol of the Triple Goddess: Maiden (or Virgin), Mother, and Crone. Inverted, it represents the male principle (the Horned God). In Western ceremonial magick (also known as high magick), the triangle symbolizes finite manifestation.

In lychnomancy, the movement, size, color, and even the sound of the candles' flames all possess special divinatory meanings.

Many modern day Witches and Wiccans perform lychnomancy as a part of their Candlemas Sabbat ritual.

M

MACHAROMANCY The art and practice of divination through knives, swords, and so forth.

An old August Eve tradition in rural Scotland is to predict the following year's marriages and deaths by throwing sickles into the air and then drawing omens from the positions in which they fall.

Many modern day Witches practice a form of macharomancy by placing a consecrated athame (a black-handled ritual knife) or dagger in the center of a circle bordered with letters and numbers. After asking the spirits a question, the athame or dagger is spun around in a spin-the-bottle fashion. Each time it stops, the letter or number its blade points to is written down. This continues until the answer is spelled out, often scrambled or in a foreign or ancient language such as Latin.

MANTIC Of, pertaining to or possessing the power of divination, or in other words, prophetic. It stems from the Greek word *manteia*, which means divination. The term *mantics* is used in the same fashion as the word suffix mancy to indicate a form of divination, and also to mean the arts of divination in general.

Other words stemming from the Greek *manteia* are mantis and mania. (In classical Greece, there existed a type of diviner called a mantis [prophet] who received his or her knowledge of future events while in a possessionlike state of frenzied ecstasy known as mania.)

MARGARITOMANCY   The art and practice of divination by pearls. The term stems from the Greek word *margarites* meaning pearls. This form of divination was a common practice in Africa, Polynesia, and the Hawaiian islands, and it was used mainly to prove whether or not an accused person was a thief.

To test for guilt, several charmed pearls would be placed under an inverted pot and then special prayers or magickal incantations would be recited. The accused person would then be made to place his or her hands on top of the pot. If the pearls began bouncing upward hitting the upside-down bottom of the pot when he or she approached or touched it, it was believed to be a definite indication of guilt.

MERKHET   A name given to a special dowsing pyramid consisting of an ellipsoidal rock suspended from an L-shaped wooden beam. It was used by priests of ancient Egypt as a device to focus energy, and as a tool for astrological calculations and land surveying while establishing the locations for sacred temples of magick and worship.

METAGNOMY   A relatively modern form of intuitive divination of the past, present, and future while under a hypnotic trance; divination by mesmerism.

Metagnomy, which began in the mid-nineteenth century, was originally used for diagnosing diseases and prescribing cures.

One of the most famous metagnomists of all times was a man named Andrew Jackson Davis (1826–1910), who was known by the nickname "The Poughkeepsie Seer."

METEOROMANCY   The art and practice of drawing omens from meteors, comets, and similar phenomena. It is related to the divinatory methods of aeromancy and roadomancy, and takes its names from the Greek word *meteoros*, which means lofty.

In ancient times, the appearance of a comet streaking across the evening sky was interpreted by diviners in some parts of the world as a sign of plague, war, fearful storms, floods, or a change in sovereignty.

METOPOMANCY (See METOPOSCOPY.)

METOPOSCOPY A form of physiognomy, metoposcopy is the art and practice of analyzing a man's or woman's character, and/or making predictions of events yet to happen, by interpreting the lines of the forehead; forehead reading.

It is also known by the name of metopomancy, which is used less often.

The diviners of ancient China were the first ones to practice the art of metoposcopy, and various methods of face reading continue to be used in modern times by a number of Asian cultures.

Aristotle was a firm believer in metoposcopy and its power to correctly analyze the human character; while the ancient Greek physician Hippocrates (the "Father of Medicine") viewed it as a legitimate science for divining the traits of future diseases.

MO A name given to an ancient system of divination practiced by Tibetan Buddhist lamas.

While holding special prayer beads known as a mala, the diviner meditates, recites a mantra, and then begins dividing the beads in a random fashion. A divinitory message is then spelled out through the number and position of the divided sections of the mala.

MOLEOSCOPY The art and practice of divining a person's character and fate by the study of moles on the human body.

For instance, a mole on the left shoulder indicates a person with a quarrelsome nature. One on the left thigh indicates a life of sorrows, while one on the right thigh indicates a life filled with good fortune. A mole on the arm between the wrist and elbow indicates a person with a happy and peaceful disposition.

This method, a variant of physiognomy, was developed by Hippocrates, the ancient Greek physician known as the Father of Medicine and the author of what is now known as the Hippocratic Oath.

Moleoscopy reached its height of popularity in the late seventeenth century with the publication of a treatise by Richard Saunders.

MOLYBDOMANCY   The art and practice of divination by molten lead. To divine fate, molten lead is dropped into a large cauldron pot filled with cold water, preferably holy water that has been blessed by a priest. The varied noises and hissings that are produced are then interpreted for special divinatory meanings, as are any symbolic shapes formed by the molten lead in the water.

The name for this method (which bears a strong similarity to the ancient egg divining method known as oomancy) is derived from the Greek word *molubdos* (meaning "lead").

Molybdomancy was a method regularly employed in the Middle Ages to divine the cause of sickness, and by Witch hunters to learn whether or not an ailing individual was the victim of bewitchment. This was carried out in the following manner: Molten lead would be held over the body of the ill person and then poured into a porringer (a small porridge bowl) containing an amount of cold water. If any image was formed by the condensing lead, it was an indication that Witchcraft was responsible for the sickness.

This method was described in both the fifteenth century Witch-hunter's handbook known as the *Malleus Maleficarum* (*The*

Witch Hammer) and in the sixteenth century's *Discoverie of Witchcraft* by Reginald Scot.

In the nineteenth century, molybdomancy was performed mainly to divine the profession of one's future husband. If the lead, after being poured into cold water, formed a shape resembling a ship, it indicated that the future husband would be a sailor. A book indicated a clergyman; a lancet (a small dual-edged surgical knife) indicated a physician; a hammer indicated a carpenter; and so forth.

This method was popular among young, unmarried women in Ireland and Wales, and it was usually carried out on Midsummer's Eve and All Hallow's Eve.

MYOMANCY   The art and practice of divination by interpreting the cries, particular activities, or sudden appearances of mice or rats, as well as by the destruction caused by them.

This method of foretelling was a common practice among diviners in ancient Egypt, Rome, and Assyria.

According to Pliny the Elder (a famous early Roman naturalist and the author of *Historia Naturalist*), the Marsian War was prognosticated by mice that gnawed the silver shields at Lanuvium, and the death of Carbo at Clusium caused by mice that gnawed the latchets of his shoes.

It is believed to be an extremely unlucky omen to observe mice or rats gnawing on or eating clothing. If they gnaw the "hangings of a room" or nibble on any piece of furniture, a death in the family is portended.

A sudden influx of mice or rats into a family's house is an indication of illness or death for a member of that family. When large numbers of mice or rats suddenly appear in the country, according to seventeenth-century Irish legend, it is an omen that war is about to break out.

The sight of mice or rats suddenly, and for no apparent reason, leaving a ship, is believed by many to presage the sinking of that vessel. When rodents suddenly flee from a house, it forebodes a disaster of some kind for the people who dwell within it, usually a fire.

In nearly all parts of the world mice and rats are thought of as the harbingers of evil and misfortune; however, in the community of Saint Combs in Scotland, mice and rats are regarded as lucky omens. According to local superstition, if they suddenly make an appearance in a house, it is a sign that the family who lives there will soon be coming into money.

n

NECROMANCY (also known as nigromancy) The ancient occult method of forecasting the future through communication with spirits of the dead; the art and practice of using dead bodies for purposes of divining.

The black art of necromancy has been practiced for thousands of years and can be traced back to ancient Greece, Rome, and Persia (now Iran). In modern times, it is a common Voodoo practice in parts of Africa, Haiti, and the southern United States.

Literally translated, necromancy means divination by the dead. It is divided into two categories: The first involves bringing the dead body back to life, while the second is concerned mainly with calling up the spirit of the dead person.

Necromantic rites, which were banned in England by the Witchcraft Act of 1604, were performed by magicians to discover the future, locate the whereabouts of hidden treasure, and to learn the nature of demons and spirits.

Traditionally, there is a special nine-day waiting period that must be observed before successful necromancy can be performed. During this time, the necromancer prepares himself for the ceremony with long hours of meditation upon death, animal sacrifices, abstaining from sex, wearing stolen grave clothes, eating unleavened black bread, and drinking unfermented grape juice. According to some grimoires, the flesh of a dog must also be consumed, as it is an animal sacred to the goddess Hecate, who presides over ghosts, death, and sorcery.

After the necessary preparations have been completed, the necromantic rite is performed in a graveyard, beginning at the first stroke of midnight. Standing in a magick circle drawn around the opened grave, the necromancer recites a series of special incantations. He then opens the coffin lid and touches the corpse thrice, commanding its disembodied spirit to reenter the dead body.

After the spirit satisfies the necromancer by giving him whatever information he had been seeking, the necromancer then rewards the spirit by giving it eternal rest. This is done by driving a wooden stake through the corpse's heart, burning the corpse, burying it in quicklime, or eating its flesh.

Famous practitioners of necromancy include the magicians John Dee and Eliphas Levi, the Greek philosopher Apollonius of Tyana, and the Witch of Endor.

NEPHELOMANCY   The art and practice of divination by interpreting the shapes of clouds and also the directions in which they move.

Since early times, man has looked to the heavens for signs from supreme beings and omens of things to come. The primitive mind viewed the clouds above, with their mysterious everchanging shapes, as messages sent by the gods.

In Rome during the time of the Roman Empire, it was the duty of the augur (a special caste of priests) to interpret the patterns of the clouds, among other things.

In some primitive cultures, the clouds themselves were believed to be the divine entities, and prayers, libations, and sacrifices of all types were made to appease them. An angry cloud god would send down his wrath in the form of destructive storms and flooding rains. However, the same clouds could also guide man by giving him symbolic messages. All man needed to do was gaze up at the clouds and learn how to properly interpret their formations.

Cloud gazing has been practiced by diviners in all parts of the world, and is related to the divinatory art of AEROMANCY (divination by air).

NINGWOT   A certain method of divination, which is performed by shamanic priests in Burma.

An ancient practice, ningwot utilizes a bamboo stem which is heated over an open fire to draw omens relating to future events. It has also been used for receiving answers (either affirmative or negative) to particular questions, and to divine the guilty.

The actual method of ningwot is a secret that is well guarded by those who practice it.

NOSTRADAMUS   A French prophet, astrologer, and physician whose world-famous prophecies have puzzled scholars and caused controversy for hundreds of years.

Nostradamus was born Michel de Nostre-Dame on December 14th, 1503 in St. Remy de Provence. During his childhood he experienced many psychic visions. He studied the Holy Qabalah, as well as astrology, astronomy, medicine, and mathematics. He possessed great healing skills and spent years in southern France treating victims of the plague.

Sometime around the age of fifty, Nostradamus began to write down the prophecies which he induced by performing a magick ritual from the *Key of Solomon* (an ancient handbook on ceremonial magick attributed to the legendary King Solomon), followed by scrying into a bowl of water.

The first collection of his prophetic visions of uncanny accuracy was written in the form of rhymed quatrains and published in the year 1555. Three years later, a second and larger

MICHEL NOSTRADAMUS.
Médecin,
Né à S.ᵗRemy, en Provence, le 14 Décemb.1503.
Mort le 2 juillet 1566.

(Fortean Picture Library)

collection of his prophecies, reaching to the year 3797, was published.

During his time, Nostradamus was admired and consulted by royalty. He had an enormous public following and enjoyed a life of fame and success until his death on July 1, 1566.

In the year 1781, the prophecies of Nostradamus were placed on the Index of Forbidden Works by the Roman Catholic Church.

NUMEROLOGY   An ancient and, at one time, sacred method of divination that analyzes the symbolism of numbers and ascribes numerical values to the letters of the alphabet.

1	2	3	4	5	6	7	8	9
A	B	C	D	E	F	G	H	I
J	K	L	M	N	O	P	Q	R
S	T	U	V	W	X	Y	Z	

By reducing birthdates, names, words, and so forth to numbers, a numerologist is able to determine one's personality traits and also divine that person's future.

In the practice of numerology, which is believed to have been created by Pythagoras, each primary number is given specific characteristics and values as well as an aspect which is either male or female. Odd numbers are regarded as masculine/active. Even numbers are feminine/passive.

To do a personal numerology reading, a person's birth chart must first be established. This is done by figuring out the three birth-name numbers and the birthdate (or Life Lesson Number).

The three birth-name numbers are comprised of the Soul Number (which is the numerical total of all the vowels in the full name), the Outer Personality Number (which is the numerical total of all the consonants in the name), and the numerical total of all the letters in the name which is known as the Path of Destiny Number.

The Soul Number reflects the true inner self, ambitions, attitudes, and feelings. The Outer Personality Number reflects health, physical appearance, and how others perceive you. The Path of Destiny Number is concerned with career, capabilities, and achievements of the past, present, and future.

The Life Lesson Number (month, date, and year of birth numerals added together and totaled until it is reduced to a single digit) is the most important number of the numerology chart for, unlike the birth-name numbers, the birthdate number can never be changed. It expresses the lessons and truths you are destined to experience throughout your lifetime.

After the four-number birth chart has been established, the numbers are interpreted in the following fashion:

The number one indicates creation, an individualist, a self-motivator, a need for freedom and independence, leadership, emotional mood swings, and a tendency to be stubborn or arrogant.

The number two indicates duality, sensitivity, a patient nature, and the ability to be objective. Oversensitivity, indecision, and inferiority complexes often present problems.

The number three indicates power, enthusiasm, energy, the ability to influence others, and a warm and expansive nature. There is a tendency to exaggerate or be self-indulgent, which should be avoided.

The number four indicates security, solidity, reliability, and a cautious nature, pride in work, and a respect for law and order. Sometimes there is a giving in to the bad habit of hoarding and/or overworking.

The number five indicates experience, sensuality, mental stimulation, versatility, a curious nature, and a strong dislike for monotony and routine jobs. There is a tendency to be insincere, which should be avoided.

The number six indicates harmony, concern, and love for people, an artistic and nurturing nature, and sometimes a tendency to be a recluse, a perfectionist, or one who permits others to take advantage of him or her.

The number seven indicates an analytical mind, psychic sensitivity, a creative imagination, a meditative nature, and an attraction to magick and the mystical. Sometimes there is a tendency to alienate loved ones.

The number eight indicates reward, justice, ambition, perseverance, and a karmic period where one reaps what he or she has sown. There is often obsession with material success and a tendency to be ruthless, which should be avoided for it will lead to a downfall.

The number nine indicates release, mental achievement, a seeker of wisdom, prophetic visions, humanitarian impulses, love and compassion for others. Self-serving interests should be avoided.

For more information, see LOVE NUMEROLOGY.

O

OCULOMANCY From the Latin *oculus* meaning the eye, oculomancy is the art and practice of divination by the eyes. It is a form of somatomancy, and has been around since ancient times.

To see a one-eyed man was once believed to be an unlucky portent. Equally as unlucky was to see a cross-eyed woman. However, to see a cross-eyed man was a lucky sign.

A man or woman having a double pupil in one eye was believed to be the harbinger of bad luck or illness by bewitchment. Such people were also thought to possess the power of the evil eye. For protection against them, the superstitious developed certain methods such as spitting on the ground (usually three times), spitting over the pinky finger, making the sign of the horns with the index and pinky fingers, or speaking to the person, which is said to break the charm.

OENOMANCY The art and practice of divination by interpreting the appearance, taste, and color of wine. It also includes divining the various symbolic patterns formed by spilt wine. For instance, if a glass of red wine should accidentally spill onto the floor, and the wine forms the shape of a heart (an obvious symbol of love), a love-related omen may be drawn from the occurrence.

In ancient Rome, oenomancy was performed by a special priestess known as a bacchante, and was ruled by the god of wine, Bacchus.

OEONISTICY (See ORNITHOMANCY.)

OGHAMIC DIVINATION   The ancient art and practice of gaining arcane knowledge based on interpreting the letters of the Celtic ogham alphabet (often designated by the names of trees). This method of divination is sometimes called the Celtic Tree Oracle.

OINOMANCY (also known as olinomancy)   The art and practice of divination by the reading of prophetic messages in the lees or dregs of wine (the sediment which settles at the bottom of a wine cask).

This method is a form of tasseography, and it was believed to have been devised by the ancient Romans.

OLINOMANCY (See OINOMANCY.)

OMEN   A name given to any phenomenon, natural event, or thing that is interpreted as a sign of good luck, misfortune, or a future event; a foreboding. The word omen is also used to mean to augur; to foreshadow by means of signs (v.t.).

From omen comes the word ominous, meaning foreboding evil or inauspicious.

Since prehistoric times, man has searched for omens in everything he sees around him—animals, birds, the elements, the earth, the heavens, his dreams, and even himself. Through omens, he could gain insight into the thing which he feared the most—the unknown. By interpreting the omens, he was able to understand his future a little more clearly, gain wisdom, be able to make the correct decisions, protect himself by taking steps to avert the portended misfortune, and be able to know the dispositions of the gods.

Omens are known by many different names, including: portents, signs, auguries, indications, tokens, harbingers, heralds, prophecies, and so forth.

OMEN DREAM   The name given to a precognitive dream containing symbols which, when properly interpreted, reveal information or warnings about a significant future event (often impending disaster, illness, or death). Some omen dreams are clearer than others, allowing the dreamer to actually see a preview of the event yet to happen.

Most people experience few, if any, precognitive dreams during the course of their lifetimes; however, some highly spiritual or psychic-sensitive persons may experience such dreams frequently.

A dream in which a clearly defined divine message is revealed to the dreamer is called an oracular dream or a prophetic dream.

OMPHALOMANCY (See OMPHILOMANCY.)

OMPHILOMANCY (also known as omphalomancy)   The art and practice of divining an individual's character and fate by interpreting the size, shape, and peculiarities of his or her navel (or belly button).

This method is regarded as a form of somatomancy, which is the divination of the bodily features in general. (For more information, see SOMATOMANCY.)

ONEIROMANCY   The scientific name for the divinatory art of interpreting the symbolic or prophetic contents of dreams, including nightmares. It is an ancient occult science that has been practiced in nearly every part of the world by Witches and non-Witches alike.

When dreams are used to gain the answer to a particular question, the method is known as dreaming true. It is based on the assumption that, during sleep, the human soul engages in spiritual intercourse with the knowing spirits.

When properly interpreted (usually through the aid of a dream dictionary), the images that dance in our heads while we are sleeping can reveal the future or warn us of impending disasters and health problems, either through actual or symbolic pictures.

Dream divination was known to have been practiced in ancient Egypt where a priestly caste arose to interpret the dreams of the pharaohs. This was done in sacred temples dedicated to the god Amun-Re.

Dream divination is also mentioned in the Bible, particularly the Old Testament.

For more information, see Further Reading.

ONOMANCY   The art and practice of divining fate by names. It is an old method popular in Europe and Great Britain during the Middle Ages and is associated with love and marriage.

If three women sharing the same name or initials sit at a table together, it indicates that one of them will be a bride before the year is through.

There are many methods for a young maiden to divine the name or initials or her future husband. A few examples are as follows: Write the names of different men on different slips of paper. Put them into a basin of water, face down, before going to bed for the night. In the morning, whichever paper is turned up will contain the name of the man you will marry. If none are turned up, it is an indication that none of those men are meant to be your husband.

Another method is to write the names on small slips of paper and roll them up in clay or pieces of soft bread pinched into balls. Place them in a basin of water, and watch for the first one to rise up. It will contain the name of your true beloved.

ONOMANTICS   The art and practice of divination by men's or women's names, an advanced form of onomancy which uses the meanings of personal names to divine an individual's character.

The basic meaning for many names can be found in baby name books and even in some larger dictionaries. Some names, such as Prudence, Faith, and Felicity, possess obvious meanings, while many other names can be translated with little effort.

ONOMATOMANCY   The art and practice of divination by interpreting the letters of a person's name. (For more information, see NUMEROLOGY.)

ONYCHOMANCY   The art and practice of divination by gazing at the reflection of sunlight on fingernails, a form of scrying.

In Arab countries, diviners at one time were known to gaze into their own polished thumbnails in order to experience clairvoyant visions. (See SCRYING.)

This method of looking into the future is still practiced in modern times by diviners in Brazil, who coat their thumbnails with a mixture of ashes and oil. After the mixture dries, its reflective surface is then gazed upon until divinatory visions become apparent.

ONYOMANCY   The art and practice of divining character and fate by interpreting the white spots on fingernails, a method related to onychomancy and regarded as a minor phase of palmistry.

Spots appearing at the bottom of the fingernails are believed to represent one's future. Spots at the middle represent the present, and spots at the top represent the past. White spots on the thumbnail predict the arrival of a present when they reach the margin. Spots on the index finger indicate that you are blessed with a true friend; on the middle finger warn of an enemy; on the ring finger reveal a new lover or marriage for you in the near future; and spots on the pinky finger indicate that you will soon embark on a journey of some sort. Fingernails that appear to have a reddish blush are said to reveal a temperamental or outspoken nature; while those of a pale pink color indicate a warm-hearted person who is very loving. Blue spots on the fingernails are said to be extremely unlucky signs, indicating misfortune of some kind or another.

OOMANCY (See OOMANTIA.)

OOMANTIA (also known as ooscopy and oomancy) The art and practice of egg divination to gain information about a child still in its mother's womb. This method, which is far from being a modern one, is traditionally performed in the following manner: To determine whether or not a pregnant woman will give birth to twins, she (or the diviner) should rub an uncooked hen's egg on her belly for a few minutes, and then break the egg open into a saucer. If it contains a single yolk, it indicates the birth of only one child; a double yolk indicates the birth of twins; a triple yolk indicates the birth of triplets. If the yolk is spotted with blood, it is a bad omen which could indicate either a miscarriage or serious complications during childbirth.

OOSCOPY (See OOMANTIA.)

OPHIOMANCY   The art and practice of divination by interpreting the appearance, behavior, biting, and hissing of snakes or serpents. Ophiomancy takes its name from the Greek word *ophis*, meaning snake.

Since biblical times, snakes have been associated with evil and the Devil, and to have one cross your path is said to be a warning of betrayal and false friends (hence the expression "snake in the grass").

Throughout the centuries, many methods of snake divination have been devised by different cultures. Some diviners mark their snakes with certain symbols, letters, or words and then place them inside a basket. The one that slithers out first, holds the correct answer.

Snake divination remains a common practice in modern times in parts of India, Egypt, China, South America, Africa, and Haiti.

Followers of certain religious cults in the United States test their faith by subjecting themselves to the bites of venomous snakes. If their faith is strong and true, they will survive the bite.

Ezekiel and a serpent. Seventeenth-century
engraving. (Publisher's Archives.)

ORACLE   A name used for a priest, priestess, or any person who transmits prophecies at a shrine consecrated to the worship and consultation of a prophetic deity.

The most famous of all oracles was the Delphic Oracle of ancient Greece, through which the god Apollo was said to have issued his prophecies and commands. She was known as the Pythia (or "Pythonness") and resided with snakes in a temple built on limestone, located approximately 100 miles from the city of Athens near Mount Parnassus. In her inner chamber at the temple (which was constructed sometime during the sixth century) the Pythia would enter a frenzied trance, and her divine utterances would be interpreted by priests who turned it into hexameter verse.

ORACLE BONE DIVINATION   Another name for the ancient art and practice of armomancy (or scapulomancy), which employs the shoulder bone of an animal, traditionally a sacrificed ox. (For more information, see ARMOMANCY.)

ORACULAR DREAM (See OMEN DREAM.)

ORDEALS   An ancient and cruel method of legal trial in which a person accused of a crime was forced to undergo extremely painful or life-threatening tests by way of determining guilt or innocence, the result being regarded as a divine judgement. Another way to define the word ordeals would be: The art and practice of guilt/innocence divination by a test of endurance.

Many women, men, and children accused of the crime of Witchcraft during the Salem Witch hysteria of 1692 were subjected to ordeals in order to prove their guilt or innocence. The most popular method of ordeals was one known as swimming. This was carried out by casting a hog-tied victim into a river. If she or he floated, it indicated guilt, and the accused was then

A suspected Witch being subjected to ordeals by immersion in water. (From *Witches Apprehended, Examined, and Executed*, a Bodleian pamphlet, London, 1613.)

condemned to death. However, if she or he sank and drowned, it was an indication of innocence.

ORNISCOPY (See ORNITHOMANCY.)

ORNITHOMANCY (also known as orniscopy and oeonisticy) The art and practice of drawing omens from the behavior of birds. For example, if a woodpecker taps on the house, a rooster crows at midnight, or a bird (especially a white one) suddenly flies into the house, it presages a death in the family.

The birds most commonly associated with omens are the raven or crow, and the eagle or the hawk.

(For more information, see ALECTRYOMANCY, AUGURY, and APANTOMANCY.)

OUIJA   A method of spirit communication consisting of a
board with the letters of the alphabet, numbers, and the words
yes and no printed on it, and a special heart-shaped pointed
called a planchette.

The term Ouija is derived from the French word *oui*, meaning yes, and the German word *ja*, which also means yes.

After a specific question is asked, a spirit guides the hands
of the querent to move the planchette around the Ouija board,
spelling out words, names, or spiritual messages.

(See also PLANCHETTE.)

OVAMANCY (also known as ovomancy)   The art and practice
of foretelling the future by dropping the white of a raw egg into
a bowl of water and then interpreting whatever symbolic shape
it assumes.

For instance, if it assumes the shape of a bell, it may mean
that a wedding will soon be taking place. A snake may indicate
the presence of an enemy or be a warning of impending danger.
If the egg white takes the shape of a boat, plane, or automobile,
it may foretell of travel in the near future.

This ancient form of egg divination was practiced in Scotland on the eve of the old Druid New Year (Samhain), in Spain
on Saint John's Eve, and in England on the last day of the year.

P

PALMIST   Another name for a palm-reader.   A person (male or female) who is skilled in the divinatory arts of cheiromancy and/or cheirognomy; a man or woman who divines by interpreting the lines of the palm and/or by the shapes of hands and fingers.

Throughout the ages, palmists have traditionally been Gypsies, village wise women, and practitioners of the Old Religion.

One of the most popular palmists of recent times was Cheiro, a flamboyant nineteenth- and early-twentieth-century palm-reader (born William Warner in County Wicklow, Ireland). He was also known by the name Count Louis le Warner de Hamon.

In London he made his fortune reading the palms of the wealthy and famous. Among his distinguished clientele were such influential figures as author Samuel Clemens (Mark Twain), Oscar Wilde, President Grover Cleveland, Edward VII, Edward VIII, and Queen Alexandra.

Cheiro died in Hollywood, California in 1936.

PALMISTRY (also known by the name of cheiromancy)   The art and practice of divination by interpreting the lines of the hand and/or by the shapes of hands and fingers; palm-reading.

Palmistry, which is believed to have originated in either China or India around the year 3000 B.C., was introduced in

Europe by the nomadic Gypsies in the fifteenth century, and it was subsequently banned by the Church.

The reading of palms is also an occult art long associated with the Craft of the Wise. (According to the ancient Tuscan legend of Aradia, the daughter of the moon goddess Diana and Lucifer was dispatched to Earth in order to introduce Witchcraft

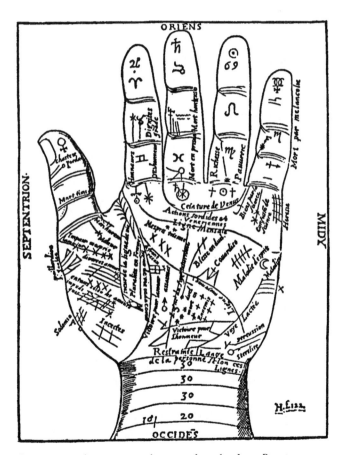

A seventeenth-century palmistry chart by Jean Baptiste Belot.

to mortals and to bestow upon them the ability to "know the secrets of the hand.")

Palmistry is divided into two aspects: cheirognomy and cheiromancy. Cheirognomy (also known as chirology) reveals a person's personality, character, and potential, while cheiromancy is the divination of the past, present, and future from what a palmist reads in the lines of the palm, fingers, and wrist.

PEGOMANCY (See HYDROMANTIA.)

PESSOMANCY   The art and practice of divination by pebbles, an ancient method of drawing omens and divining fate.

In the countries of Scotland and Wales, it was a Pagan custom at one time for persons to cast a white pebble bearing their name into the All Saints Eve bonfire known as the Coel Coeth. Special prayers would be recited, and then in the morning, after the fire had died out, the pebbles would be checked to see if any were missing from the ashes. Any person whose name was inscribed on a missing pebble was believed to be destined to fall ill or die within the ensuing twelve months.

PHRENOLOGY   The relatively modern psychic science of interpreting a man's or woman's personality and/or mental capability by means of interpreting the conformation of the skull; also known as head-reading.

This system was formulated by Franz Joseph Gall in the late eighteenth century. In the year 1836, a phrenology museum and publishing house was opened by the famous Fowler family in New York City. They founded the monthly *American Phrenological Journal*, which contained news about the arts of phrenology and physiology, among other topics. Eventually the American Institute of Phrenology was established.

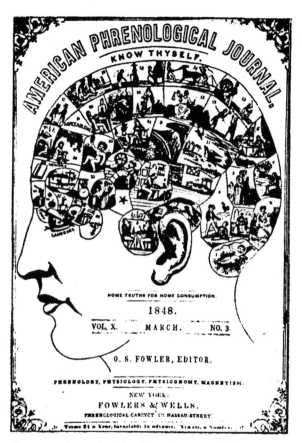

The cover from the March 1848 issue of *American Phrenological Journal* (From *Heads and Headlines: The Phrenological Fowlers* by Madeleine B. Stern, University of Oklahoma Press, 1971.)

Phrenology enjoyed popular appeal, but it was later discredited by scientific research. Interest in it subsided in the United States in the 1930s.

PHRENOPATHY   The art and practice of divination by means of inducing an altered state of consciousness in which the subject becomes clairvoyant and is able to perceive future events or hidden knowledge; the act of creating a state of heightened psychic awareness in an individual through hypnotism.

PHYLLORHODOMANCY   The art and practice of divination by roses. This method, which originally consisted of slapping rose petals against the hand and then interpreting the loudness of the sound, was a popular (if not unusual) form of divination among the ancient Greeks. They used it for determining the success or failure of their undertakings.

Rose divination was ruled by the love goddess Aphrodite, to whom the rose was a sacred flower.

In the eighteenth and nineteenth centuries, diviners in England employed the rose in various ways in the popular art of love divination, usually to discover one's future husband. The most common method for this was to pluck a rose on Midsummer's Eve, wrap it in white paper, and then put it away in some secret place. On Christmas Day, the rose was removed from the paper and worn (preferably on one's bosom). The first man to take it from the wearer would be the one destined to marry her.

To test if your lover has remained faithful to you, gather a rose on Midsummer's Eve and then keep it wrapped in white paper until Christmas Day. If its red color has faded, it indicates that your lover has been untrue.

PHYSIOGNOMY   The art and practice of personal character analysis, diagnosing illnesses, or divining fate by interpreting the physical appearance of the facial features. Its practice dates back to ancient Greece, and a form of it (mainly the observation of men's and women's facial similarities to certain animals) appeared in the *History of Animals* by the philosopher Aristotle.

In modern China, physiognomy is regarded as an adjunct of medicine. The shape of the face is analyzed, and the features are checked for balance and proportion. (A "balanced" face is found on a man or woman of strong character. It is also an indication of a bright and successful future.) Over one hundred facial areas are observed and compared using a special physiognomy chart in order for the face-reader to arrive at an accurate conclusion.

PLANCHETTE   A triangular pointer that is used to spell out spirit-guided messages on a Ouija board when touched by the fingertips of one or more persons or spiritualist mediums. With a pencil attached, the planchette can also be used for automatic writing.

PODOMANCY (also known as solistry)   The art and practice of divination by interpretation of the lines on the soles of the feet. This is a method similar to palmistry, and at one time it was popular throughout China.

Like the reading of palms, podomancy is distantly related to astrology and is based on a system in which particular meanings are associated with certain features of the human foot, such as size, shape, and lines.

It has been said that feet are the "symbol of the soul" and are believed to reveal both a person's character and future when properly interpreted.

PORTEND (See PORTENT.)

PORTENT   An omen or a prophetic sign, especially one that is ominous or evil.

To portend (v.t.) is to foretell or to be an omen.

These words stem from the Latin *portendere*, which means to foretell.

PRECOGNITION   The paranormal or extrasensory perception of future events, usually through dreams or visions; a psychic awareness of the future.

PREDICTION   A foretelling of the future by means of divination, astrology, precognition, or omens of any kind.

Some diviners use psychic methods such as clairvoyance and automatic writing to obtain their predictions, while others prefer working with mantic objects and tools like fortune telling cards, rune stones, and pendulums to do the same.

Predictions can be made while one is meditating, in a state of trance, channeling a spirit guide or communicating directly with gods or goddesses, and also while in the dream state.

Predictions arrived at through dream interpretation or by the guidance of deities through dreams were methods regularly employed by the ancient Egyptians, and also mentioned a number of times throughout the Bible, such as in Numbers 12:5–6 and Daniel 2:2 and 4:7. (For more information on dream divination, see ONEIROMANCY.)

The ability to make predictions is not limited to any specific religious practice or culture, and throughout the course of history both men and women (and children as well) from all walks of life have made predictions through various means of prognosticating the future.

Among the most well-known prediction-makers of the twentieth century whose successful predictions have been documented are Edgar Cayce, Jeane Dixon, and Sydney Omarr.

PREMONITION   A psychic sense or intuitive feeling about future events before they happen; presage. (Also known as a presentiment.)

PRESAGE   An intuitive feeling that indicates or warns of a future occurrence; to predict the future or foretell an event before it happens.

PRESENTIMENT   Another word for premonition.

PROGNOSTICATION   The occult art and practice of divining future events by using omens and/or psychic feelings as a guide. PROGNOSTICATE: To predict events that are yet to take place by interpreting present indications. PROGNOSTIC: This is a sign or omen of an event, either good or bad, which is yet to happen.

PROPHECY (noun)   The outcome of any type of divination; a prediction made by a prophet; a foretelling of future events or a revelation of a divine being's will.

PROPHESY (verb transitive)   To predict the future; to speak as a prophet; or to utter by divine inspiration.

PROPHET   A word used to describe a gifted person who speaks as the interpreter, through whom a divinity expresses its will; a soothsayer or predictor; a person who receives symbolic spiritual messages from a god or goddess; an inspired teacher or revealer of the Divine Will.

PROPHETESS   A female prophet.

PSYCHOGRAPHOLOGY The art and practice of divination by handwriting. Unlike graphology, which analyzes the peculiarities of an individual's handwriting, psychographology interprets a person's personality traits and physical appearance, along with their past, present, and future, by psychic impressions received when placing a hand upon their handwriting.

The most famous psychographologist in history was a man by the name of Raphael Schermann, who was born in Krakow, Poland in 1879. His special talent was successfully used to aid law enforcement officials in solving a murder case in New York City.

PSYCHOGRAPHY The art and practice of divining future events, gaining arcane knowledge, or receiving answers to questions through the clairvoyant or spirit-guided act of writing or drawing on a piece of paper while in an altered state of consciousness; divination by automatic writing.

The word psychography is also used to describe the phenomenon of spirit-written messages which mysteriously appear on photographic film.

PSYCHOMANCY According to John Gaule's seventeenth-century work *Mysmantia*, the art and practice of divination "by men's souls, affections, wills, and religious or moral dispositions."

PSYCHOMETRY (also known as hylomancy) The art and practice of receiving psychic impressions of a person by concentrating on their photograph and/or by holding a physical object that has been in their possession. It is based on the belief that a human being's personal objects are energized with his or her vibrations. When these personal objects are held in the hands of a psychic-sensitive person, the vibrations can be tuned in and divined.

Psychometry is a psychic/divinatory art popular among many modern Witches, and it is frequently used by psychic detectives, usually to locate missing persons, either dead or alive, and to describe crime scenes and other details relating to a particular case.

PYROMANCY (also known as pyroscopy)   The art and practice of divination through the interpretation of the color, shape, and intensity of a fire into which sacred herbs, twigs, or incense have been cast.

Another method of pyromancy was to throw peas into a fire. If they burned quickly, it was interpreted as a favorable omen. When a sacrificial fire was used, the practice of divination was called empyromancy.

PYROSCOPY (See PYROMANCY.)

R

RABDOMANCY (See RHABDOMANCY.)

RADIESTHESIA   The art and practice of divination by means
of a pendulum.
    To make and use a pendulum, attach a small weight (such as
a quartz crystal, ring, key, etc.) to a string or lightweight chain.
Hold it perfectly still in your right hand, while you concentrate
on a specific question. If the pendulum begins to rotate in a
clockwise motion, it indicates an affirmative answer. If it rotates
counterclockwise, it indicates a negative response.
    To determine the sex of an unhatched egg, hold a pendulum
above the egg and concentrate. If the pendulum continuously
swings towards and away from you, it indicates male; laterally,
it indicates female. No movement whatsoever indicates an un-
fertilized egg.
    Map dowsing is a popular form of radiesthesia, using a pen-
dulum and a large map to find missing persons, buried treasure,
underground water, lost objects, and so forth. This method of
divination reached its height of popularity in the early 1900s.
    In the year 1947, the body of a missing mountain climber
was found in the Alps after a French diviner named Francois
Gramenia used the map dowsing method to locate the exact
spot where the young man had fallen to his death. His successful employment of divination not only won him worldwide ac-

claim and a reward of 50,000 francs, it also helped prove to the world that the often scoffed at art of radiesthesia is indeed a credible occult science.

Although radiesthesia is popular among many modern diviners, including New Age healers who use the interpretations of a pendulum's motion to indicate the presence of a disease, the use of the pendulum dates back to ancient times.

According to the records of the Byzantine historian Marcellinus, numerous diviners had been arrested and executed for the crime of using a suspended ring and a circle of alphabetical letters to divine the name of Emperor Valens' successor.

RHABDOMANCY   The art and practice of divination by wand, rod, or wooden stick. (The name of this particular form of divination comes from the Greek word *rhabdos*, meaning a rod.)

Some rhabdomancers draw omens by marking special divination sticks with symbols or names, casting them into a vessel, and then interpreting the first one drawn out. Another method is to cast the sticks into the air and then to interpret the position in which they fall. (See BELOMANCY and also CLEROMANCY.)

RHAPSODOMANCY   Similar to bibliomancy, it is the art and practice of divination by books of poetry or song lyrics. A book is opened to a page selected at random, and the first line that comes to view is interpreted as prophetic.

This ancient method draws its name from the Greek word *rhapsodia*, meaning rhapsody.

In modern times, rhapsodomancers have been known to employ radios instead of books of poetry to reveal the unknown or to gain insight. This is done simply by concentrating for awhile on whatever matter is at hand, and then turning on a radio. The lyrics and/or the title of whatever song is being played at that moment are then analyzed for hidden meanings.

ROADOMANCY   The art and practice of divination by interpretation of the stars.

A falling or shooting star is believed to be a sign that a child has just come into the world. The shooting star falls over the spot where the baby is born, according to nineteenth-century folklore.

Many believe that a wish made quickly and with sincerity on the first star of the evening, or while a falling star streaks across the nighttime sky, will be granted. This old belief is evident in the popular children's rhyme which is supposed to be recited with eyes closed after seeing such a star: "Starlight, star bright, First star that I've seen tonight. Wish I may, wish I might, grant the wish I wish tonight."

Twelfth-century engraving. (Publisher's Archives)

To some, a falling star is also said to be an unlucky sign for those who witness it, a presage of death (especially of a king or other man of great power), or an indication that someone close to you has just passed on.

RUNES   Ancient Norse and Teutonic mystical symbols possessing great divinatory and magickal properties. They are carved, etched, or painted upon pieces of clay, stone or wood, and are used for divination and spiritual growth. The word rune stems from *ru*, an Indo-European root meaning secret or mystery.

Popularized as an oracle in the late twentieth century, a typical set of runes are made up of two dozen rune-stone tiles that are cast in lots, in a manner similar to the *I Ching*, or laid out for a reading like fortune-telling cards.

In ancient times, rune stones were simply small pebbles or flat pieces of wood etched with certain occult symbols. They were cast upon the ground to both divine the future and to evoke the powers of the great gods and goddesses of the pre-Christian Norse religion.

The art of rune casting was ruled by the god Odin, who, according to mythology, was the creator of the runes.

Rune divination originated in Northern Europe around the time of the Vikings in Scandinavia. It was widespread in all Nordic and Germanic lands by the year A.D. 100, and was at its height in Europe, Russia, and Great Britain during the Dark Ages. In the year 1639, a Church edict banned their use.

There are three main types of runes: Anglo-Saxon, Germanic, and Scandinavian. Their variations and subdivisions include the Druidic Ogam Bethluisnion, Egyptian hieroglyphics, Theban Script, Pictish, Celestial, Malachim, and Passing the River.

SAGA   A term used in the Middle Ages for a diviner.

SCAPULOMANCY (See ARMOMANCY.)

SCIOMANCY   The art and practice of divination by shadows or through spirit aid. The most common method was to observe the size, shapes, and changing appearance of shadows of the dead, thus drawing a prophetic conclusion.

A bad omen is portended for anybody who casts a headless shadow (or no shadow at all) on the eve of Yule or Hoshana Rabba. According to legend, that person will lose their life within the course of the year.

SCRYING   The art and practice of interpreting the unknown (including past, present, and future) from images seen while gazing into a crystal ball, candle flame, pool of water, gazing mirror, or other speculum; crystal gazing; mirror gazing.

The term scrying is derived from the old English word *descry*, meaning "to perceive from a distance; to discover by the eye." It is known throughout the world and takes many forms. (See HYDROMANCY and HYDROMANTIA.)

Scrying, usually by gazing into a crystal ball or a black cauldron filled with water, is a popular practice among many modern-day Witches, and it is a tradition which is carried out by many Wiccans on the night of the Samhain Sabbat (Halloween).

SEANCE   A gathering of persons to contact and receive messages from discarnate beings or spirits of the dead, often for gaining insight into the future or the unknown. Traditionally, a seance is held in the dark or by candlelight at a table where all persons attending are seated with hands joined together to form a circle. At all seances, at least one medium must be present to serve as a channel for communications.

SECOND SIGHT   A name given to the ability to perceive that which is unknown through the gift or talent of clairvoyance. Persons who are born with or who, at some point in their life, develop second sight are often able to experience psychic visions of the past, present, and future.

Second sight often occurs when one is dreaming or in a meditational state or trance. Sometimes it can be voluntarily induced. Other times it can occur without warning in the waking state, in the form of "hallucinatory" visions.

In the Middle Ages, many persons with second sight (or those who were even suspected or possessing it) were condemned as sorcerers and executed for being in league with the Devil. Insanity and demonic possession were also attributed to those with second sight in unenlightened times.

SELENOMANCY   The art and practice of divination by the phases and appearances of the moon, a practice of the utmost antiquity.

There are countless moon-related omens that have evolved since prehistoric times. For instance, the moon has long been used to divine the fate of individuals at the time of their birth. If a child is born when the moon is one day old, he or she will be blessed with wealth and longevity. A child born during the waning phase of the moon will be unhealthy. A child born when the moon is full will be blessed with strength; however, a child born during the dark of the moon will need special care and will probably die before reaching puberty.

In ancient Assyria, diviners interpreted the appearance of a halo or ring around the moon as an omen of a forthcoming siege. However, a break in it indicated a happy escape. The shape of the moon's "horns" were also observed, as were the moon's brightness and color.

Selenomancy takes its name from *Selene*, the Greek goddess of the waxing moon. (In ancient Greece, she was the deity who presided over this particular form of divination.)

SHEW-STONE   A nickname given to a flat, circular, black stone with a highly polished surface. It is used by scryers in the same manner as a crystal ball, to divine the future or the past.

Ideally a shew-stone is gazed upon by candlelight or moonlight after a period of quiet meditation. The stone should be tilted to catch the light source and also to prevent the scryer from gazing directly at his or her own reflection on its surface. When the answers to whatever questions asked are ready to be revealed to the scryer, they will be perceived by means of clairvoyance.

Dr. John Dee, the acclaimed British astrologer, psychic, and scryer, was known to often use a shew-stone when he divined the future and provided consultation to Queen Elizabeth I of England and to other clients of nobility. The shew-stone he used was a black mirror made from the gemstone called obsidian.

Along with Dee's other metaphysical objects and tools of the trade, his shew-stone is currently on display at the British Museum.

SIDEROMANCY   The art and practice of divination by throwing an odd number of straws upon a red-hot iron and drawing omens from the twisting and bending of the burning straws, the intensity of the flames, and/or the course of the smoke.

Sideromancy was a popular practice among the ancient Romans, who sometimes substituted crushed beans and peas in place of the straws.

The following methods of divination are considered to be variations of the art of sideromancy: capnomancy, causimomancy, critomancy, daphnomancy, libanomancy, and pyromancy.

SIGN (See OMEN.)

SIGNIFICATOR   The name given to a card (usually one from a Tarot deck) which is used in a reading to represent the man or woman whose future is being divined. (For more information, see CARTOMANCY, CELTIC CROSS, TAROT.)

SOLISTRY (See PODOMANCY.)

SOMATOMANCY (also known as characterology)   The art and practice of divination of character from bodily features. It takes its name from the Greek word *soma*, which means a body, and is believed to have originated over five thousand years ago in China.

A few examples of the methods which can be classified under the heading of somatomancy are: palmistry (cheiromancy and cheirognomy), physiognomy (face-reading), and phrenology (the reading of heads or skulls).

Since early times, people throughout the world have naturally associated human behavior and personality traits with physical attributes (overweight people are supposed to be jolly, beady-eyed people cannot be trusted, women with blonde hair are dumb, and so forth). This bent of mind is illustrated by folk legends, literary traditions, everyday thinking, and even some modern day scientific theories.

The reading of an individual's character and fate is mentioned in the Bible (e.g. Matt. 6:22–23), and during the Middle Ages and the Renaissance the various arts of somatomancy were studied by numerous savants, including many well-known and respected men of science. (The Swiss philosopher and theologian, Johann Kaspar Lavater was perhaps the most famous pre-nineteenth-century physiognomist.)

Somatomancy reached the height of its popularity in the nineteenth century. Afterwards, major interest in it subsided.

SORTILEGE (See LOT CASTING.)

SORTITION (See LOT CASTING.)

SPATALAMANCY The art and practice of divination by means of interpreting the skin, the bones, and/or the excrement of both man and beast, a method which originated in ancient times.

SPECULUM A name used for a crystal ball or other object possessing a shiny, reflective surface that is used in scrying as an object to focus one's gaze in entering a state of trance consciousness.

SPLANCHOMANCY The ancient art and practice of divining fate by examining the entrails of persons who had been sacrificed to a particular god or goddess. A similar method, anthropomancy, was the reading of omens from the entrails of sacrificed children (and sometimes women).

This form of divination was common in ancient times among many cultures, most notably the Greeks and the Celtic priests known as Druids.

SPODOMANCY   The art and practice of divination by interpreting cinders or soot, originally from sacrificial fires.

In the Middle Ages, prophetic messages were read in the following way from cinders that jumped from the hearth: Hollow, oblong cinders were known as coffins, and they indicated a coming death in the family. Oval cinders were called cradles and indicated the advent of a child. Round ones were called purses, and they indicated prosperity. Heart-shaped ones were the sign of a lover.

If a clot of soot fell down the chimney during a wedding breakfast, according to an old Scottish superstition, it was a portent of ill luck for the newlywed couple.

STERNOMANCY (From the Greek word *sternon* meaning the chest) The art and practice of divination by the breastbone (or sternum) of animals or humans, often victims of sacrifice.

The flat narrow bone to which the first seven ribs are attached is inspected by the diviner, who looks for significant peculiarities and markings from which prophetic messages may be obtained. The size and shape of the breastbone is also taken into consideration, as is the way in which it burns when placed in a fire.

The old holiday custom of two persons pulling a turkey or chicken wishbone until it breaks into two parts is actually a remnant of sternomancy.

STICHOMANCY (See BIBLIOMANCY.)

STOLISOMANCY   The art and practice of divination by interpreting certain peculiarities of dress. For instance, accidentally wearing a shirt inside out is said to be an omen of bad luck throughout the entire day, while putting on a dress the wrong way portends that you will soon get a new dress or someone will present you with a gift. Another example of stolisomancy is: If your right shoelace becomes untied, it is believed to be an indication that someone you know is speaking kindly of you. If your left shoelace becomes untied, something bad is being said about you behind your back.

SYCOMANCY   The art and practice of divination by the leaves of a fig tree.

This method was performed by writing messages on the leaves and then observing them as they dried. The longer it took for the leaves to dry, the more favorable the omen.

A modern form of sycomancy involves various messages written on slips of paper, rather than fig leaves. They are rolled up and then held in a strainer over a steaming pot of water. The slip of paper which unrolls first will give the correct message. However, in order for this method to work properly (according to occult tradition), one of the rolled up slips of paper must remain blank.

T

TAGHAIRM (See TARBFEIS.)

TARBFEIS   An Old Irish word meaning bull feast and used to describe the old Celtic practice of drinking the blood and consuming the meat of a properly sacrificed bull, and then sleeping in its warm hide in order to induce prophetic dreams. The Druids believed that by doing so, they could somehow transfer the strength of the animal to themselves. In order to work properly, this method of divination had to be carried out during the correct phase of the moon and at a sacred site that was inhabited by spirits.

Divination through bull sacrifices were commonly performed by the Druid priests of ancient times. When not at war, they would sacrifice a pair of white bulls. However, when they were engaged in battle, they would sacrifice their captured enemies (usually by burning them alive in huge wicker structures and then interpreting the fire, the smoke, and the cries of their sacrificial offerings.)

A method similar to tarbfeis was taghairm. This is an early Celtic form of divination by means of sleeping in the fresh hide of a correctly sacrificed ox in order to induce prophetic dreams and gain occult knowledge.

TAROT   A deck of seventy-eight cards used for reading the past, the future, and fortunes. It is divided into two parts: the

Seventeenth-century illustration depicting humans being sacrificed by Druid priests. (Aylett Sammes, *Britannia Antiqua Illustrata*, 1676.)

Minor Arcana and the Major Arcana. The Minor Arcana consists of fifty-six divinatory cards divided into four suits of fourteen cards each: Swords, Pentacles, Wands, and Cups. The Major Arcana consists of twenty-two highly symbolic trump cards with colorful allegorical figures.

The various methods of Tarot card reading include the Celtic Cross method, the Golden Dawn method (modified by the late Aleister Crowley), and the Oracles of Julia Orsini, which is an ancient French method that uses a significator card plus forty-two other cards.

The Tarot is perhaps the number one method of divination among most Wiccans, modern Witches, and Neo-Pagans, and its popularity has extended far beyond the traditional occult community. Tarot cards and books abound in bookshops and gift shops; Tarot classes are offered at many colleges; Tarot how-to videos can be obtained at some public libraries; there are special Tarot decks designed for feminists; cat lovers, and Renaissance aficionados; and there are even 900 phone services in operation that offer Tarot card readings for a fee.

There exist many varied theories as to the origin of the Tarot. Eliphas Levi (a popular nineteenth-century occultist and author) believed that they derived their mysterious name from the legendary Egyptian *Book of Thoth* since *Tar Ro* (which translates into Royal Pathway) were thought to be the Egyptian words for Book of Thoth.

Some researchers have linked the cards to the Tarot river valley in the northern region of Italy, while others have traced them to the Egyptian or Chaldean ancestors of the Gypsies. However, the exact origin and purpose of the Tarot remains a mystery to this day.

Given seventy-eight cards, each having many different meanings (depending also upon where in the spread the card is turned up) allowing for each card's reversed meaning, the many methods of reading the Tarot, and the numerous decks that exist (each possessing its own presentation and interpretation of the symbols), it would be next to impossible to give accurate details on how to read Tarot cards without devoting an entire book to the subject.

Different decks usually come equipped with their own set of card reading instructions/interpretations, or a companion book, which may or may not have to be purchased separately.

Another factor in becoming a Tarot reader is that not all decks are perfect for all readers. You may have to experiment by working with a number of decks before you find one that harmonizes with your own distinct divinatory energies and one with which you feel the most comfortable doing readings.

Having to learn and memorize both the upright and reversed meanings of each of the seventy-eight different cards in

ROY DE COUPE   REYNE D'EPEE

(The New York Public Library)

the average Tarot deck can amount to a mind-boggling undertaking for the novice card reader. Luckily, there are a few good
decks designed especially for beginners. These decks have the
meanings of each card printed right on them. This certainly
makes it a lot easier and less time-consuming to read the cards
than having to pause throughout the reading in order to look up
the meaning of each card in a book.

In addition to divination, the Tarot can also be used as a
powerful tool of magick to achieve positive results, and many
modern day Witches who divine with them can also spell cast
with them.

A basic Tarot spell consists of lighting candles (of the appropriate magickal color)—meditating upon a card which cor-

responds to the spell being performed—and the recitation of an incantation. For instance, a Tarot love spell would be performed with pink candles and The Lovers card; a spell for spiritual enlightenment would use yellow or orange candles and The Sun card; and so forth.

For those of you who are interested in the magickal workings of the Tarot, I highly recommend the following books: *Magick and the Tarot* by Tony Willis, (Published by Aquarian Press, England, 1988) and also *Tarot Spells* by Janina Renee and *The New Golden Dawn Ritual Tarot* by Chic and Sandra Tabatha Cicero (both published in 1991 by Llewellyn Publications of St. Paul, Minnesota.)

(The New York Public Library)

The following companies offer free catalogs featuring a wide variety of Tarot decks from which to choose:

Abyss Distribution (800-326-0804)
Llewellyn (800-843-6666)
U.S. Games Systems (800-544-2637)

For more information, see Further Reading.

TAROTOLOGY   The unofficial name for the art and practice of divination by interpreting the messages contained in Tarot cards. Tarot divination can also be classified under the heading of cartomancy (divination by fortune-telling or playing cards).

In Europe, playing cards were originally designed for drawing omens (not game playing), and Tarot-like divination cards were known to exist in the country of China prior to the year A.D. 1000.

For more information, see TAROT and CARTOMANCY.

TASSEOGRAPHY   The art and practice of divination by interpretation of the symbolic patterns made by tea leaves in a cup; also known as tea-leaf reading.

Although generally associated with Gypsy fortune-tellers, the practice of reading tea leaves dates back thousands of years to the country of China where it was developed into a mystical science.

With a little imagination and a bit of practice, you can divine with tea leaves for yourself or for others. For best results, use China tea or an excellent grade of tea containing a minimum of tea dust. And be sure to always use a nondecorated teacup, preferably white.

For each cup to be read, put a teaspoon and a half of loose tea (not teabags) in a teapot. Add boiling water, stir vigorously, and allow the mix to stand for three minutes before filling your cup. The person whose fortune is being told must drink the entire cup of tea until there is just enough liquid remaining to barely cover the leaves.

If you are right-handed, pick up the cup by the handle with your left hand. If you are left-handed, pick it up with your right hand. (The reason for this is because the left side is believed to be the psychic side if you are a right-handed person, and vice versa.) Gently move the cup in a clockwise circular motion. Do this seven continuous times, and then place it back in its saucer.

Gaze into the bottom of the cup. Relax and concentrate on the patterns produced by the wet tea leaves until you determine what symbolic shape the leaves have formed. And always be on the lookout for significant numbers, initials, and/or astrological symbols that might appear in or around the main pattern, as they often play an important role in the interpretation of the tea leaves.

For more information, see Further Reading.

TEPHRAMANCY The art and practice of drawing omens from ashes, usually of a burned tree trunk. To spell out a divinatory message, diviners look for symbols in the ashes, much in the same way that a tasseographer observes the tea leaves in the bottom of a cup.

The types of trees used most often by diviners are the alder, bay, elder, hazel, oak, rowan, and willow. All are connected to the Old Religion and the magickal arts in one way or another.

The burning of elder sticks in a Christmas Eve fire was at one time believed by many to reveal the true identity of anyone who practiced the black art of sorcery; the guilty person's initials, name, or even an image of his or her face supposedly would appear in the ashes.

TERAPHIM A name given to mysterious gemstone amulets that were fashioned in the shape of human beings or divine beings. They were believed to possess abundant magickal power, and were worn by ancient Hebrews for the purpose of divining events of the future. (See also URIM AND THUMMIM.)

THEOMANCY   The art and practice of divination by consultation of spirits or divine beings.

The oldest and most popular method of theomancy is probably the seance, which is a gathering of persons to contact and receive messages from discarnate beings or spirits of the dead. A seance is held in the dark, or by candlelight, at a table where all persons attending are seated with hands joined together to form a circle. At all seances, at least one medium must be present to serve as a channel for communications.

THERIOMANCY   The art and practice of divination by the observance of wild beasts and their behavior.

This method of prophecy is linked to the ancient belief in theriomorphism (gods, goddesses, or other divine beings who inhabit the bodies of animals, or who can appear in animal form at will).

Theriomancy is one of the oldest forms of prophecy, dating back to the days of early man. Involving various animals, birds, and even insects, it has been practiced in all parts of the world by every culture, and continues to be used in modern times as a means to predict events of the future, answer questions, determine good or bad omens, and even forecast the weather.

Every year on the second day of February, the shadow of a groundhog on Groundhog Day (which incidentally coincides with the Wiccan Sabbat of Candlemas) is believed to determine the number of weeks of winter weather that lies ahead. This curious event is actually a form of theriomantic divination!

Other methods of divination considered to be related to theriomancy include alectryomancy, apantomancy, felidomancy,

An illustration from Schedel's
World Chronicle, 1493.

hippomancy, myomancy, ophiomancy, ornithomancy, and zoomancy.

TIROMANCY   The art and practice of divination by cheese and also by its coagulation.

In days of yore, young maidens in rural villages would divine the names of their future husbands or lovers by writing the names of all possible suitors on top of separate pieces of cheese. The man whose name was on the piece of cheese that grew mold first was believed to be the ideal love mate. (This unusual and certainly unromantic method of love divination also worked just as well for the opposite sex.)

Another way to divine the names was to write them on separate pieces of cheese and then place them inside a cage along with a hungry mouse or rat. Whichever piece he ate first would give the desired indication. (This method was also used to determine guilt as well as fidelity, and to give yes or no answers to questions.)

TRANSATAUMANCY   The art and practice of divination by interpreting events heard or witnessed by accident.

This form of divination, which is believed to have been practiced by both the ancient Egyptians and Romans, covers a broad range of omens and visions that are accidentally experienced by a woman, man, or child. Chance remarks that are overhead in a crowd of people and then utilized in a prognosticative manner is one example of transataumancy that continues to be practiced by many people in contemporary times.

The clairvoyant art of knowing what another person will say just before they actually say it is considered to be a form of transataumancy. It is known as cledonomancy, and is not regarded as a common ability. Many diviners who possess this rare and special psychic gift interpret the statements they knew would be said to draw omens about future events, usually quite successfully.

TUPHRAMANCY (See (TEPHRAMANCY.)

TYROMANCY (See TIROMANCY.)

उ

URIM AND THUMMIM   The most famous of all lots, these were sacred amulets designed for divination purposes. Made from small pebbles or pieces of wood, they were carried in a small pouch inside the breastplate of the High Priests of Israel and used for the reading of oracles.

The reading of the Urim and Thummim was included in the duties of the High Priest. The oracle was consulted only for matters which concerned the fate of the community, and it was considered taboo to consult it for any matter of a personal nature.

The origin of the Urim and Thummim can be traced back to the ancient Babylonian religion, but as to the precise method of using the oracles, this is a matter that remains shrouded in mystery to this very day.

UROMANCY   The art and practice of divination by the inspection of human or animal urine.

In the sixteenth and seventeenth centuries, it was a common practice to test for Witchcraft by placing iron nails, pins, needles, or half horseshoes in a bottle filled with urine from the woman or man accused of the crime, and then stopping it up with a cork. If the suspected Witch or Warlock suddenly fell ill or if the cork popped out of the bottle on its own accord, it was taken as a sign of guilt from God.

Another method of Witch detection popular in Europe was to bake a special cake, loaf, or wafer containing a bit of urine and hair from a person who was believed to have been victimized by bewitchment. According to *Hesperides* (a mid-seventeenth-century work by Robert Herrick), this was "another to bring in the Witch." (The special "Witchcake" was either burned, buried in the ground, or fed to the suspected Witch with his or her reactions observed and used for the required indication.)

Since the time of ancient Rome, urine has been observed in order to give a clue to the future. One popular method was to look for bubbles in the chamberpot after making water. If any were present, this was an indication that one would soon be receiving a large sum of money.

V

VIRGILIAN LOTS   An ancient form of bibliomancy involving randomly selected passages from the written works of the Roman poet Virgil, which are then interpreted to reveal future events or to answer a specific personal question.

This method originated in Italy (where it was known as *sortes Virgiliana*), and although all of the works of Virgil have been divined, the most popular one was, and still remains, the *Aeneid*—an epic which retold the fall of Troy and wove a tale of sea adventure similar to the wanderings of Odysseus.

The *Aeneid* was considered to be an allegory of sacred things, and in Virgil's fourth *Eclogue*, the second coming of Jesus Christ was said to have been prophesied.

In the medieval era, the works of Virgil gained a new popularity; not for the poetry, but rather for the author's supposed knowledge of the black arts.

VISION   An altered state of consciousness in which a sacred or prophetic image is perceived; a mental image that appears to one in a dream, while in a trance, or while scrying. A woman, man, or child who is gifted with this paranormal vision is called a visionary.

Unlike other methods of omen reading, which can be acquired and perfected by means of training and practice, vision divination is usually an ability that one is given at the time of birth. It is usually handed down from generation to generation, and many consider it to be a gift from God or from the Goddess.

It is also very common for a traumatic incident such as an automobile accident, coma, or near-death experience to trigger the ability to receive visions.

Historically, many famous visionaries have become great prophets, royal advisers, spiritual leaders, and even saints; however, in the not-too-distant past, most people who claimed to have seen divinatory visions were looked upon with fear and misunderstanding. Their special talents were attributed by skeptics to fraud, mental illness, or even demonic possession.

VITKA   Rune mistress; a Pagan priestess or seeress who divines the future by casting rune stones into a circle drawn on the ground and then interpreting the patterns formed by the stones.

VULCANOSCOPY (also known as vulcanomancy)   The art and practice of drawing omens from volcanoes and their eruptions. The name of this occult science derives from the Latin *Vulcanus*, meaning god of fire, and it has been practiced by diviners since primitive times in all parts of the world where volcanoes exist.

VULPESOMANCY   The art and practice of divination by observing the behavior of foxes. This form of divination (which takes its name from the Latin *vulpes*, meaning fox) is a common practice in West Africa where the sand fox is considered to be an animal of abundant magickal power.

At sunset, rectangular grids are traced in the desert sand and then filled in with special symbols which represent the diviner's questions. (These usually pertain to matters of healing, fertility, and farming.) Peanuts are scattered around the grids to attract the foxes, and then at dawn their tracks left in the sand are interpreted.

ण

WATER WITCH A nickname used to describe a man or woman who uses a divining rod to locate underground water; a dowser. (For more information, see DOWSING.)

XYLOMANCY The art and practice of drawing omens from twigs, pieces of wood, or fallen tree branches by interpreting their shapes and formations. It also pertains to divination by observing the position of logs as they burn in a fire.

Other forms of divination related to xylomancy are dendromancy (divination by oak trees) and tephramancy (divination by the ashes of a burned tree trunk).

Tree divination no doubt has its roots (pardon the pun) in the primitive practice of tree worship, which is the earliest form of religion.

YIN AND YANG In the Chinese divinatory system of the
I Ching (*Book of Changes*), there are two kinds of lines which make
up the sixty-four vertical six-line columns known as hexagrams:
yin lines and yang lines.

The yin lines are broken lines denoting earth, darkness, female energy, passiveness, the negative, and the corporeal. The
yang lines are solid lines denoting heaven, light, male energy,
aggression, the positive, and the spiritual.

Yin and yang, which are the basis for the *I Ching*, are opposite but always complementary and necessary to each other.
They symbolize the universal life force which is in a constant
ebb and flow; contending, yet in harmony; and perpetually
flowing into each other in stately cosmic rhythm. (For more information see *I CHING*.)

The ancient symbol of Yin and Yang.

134

Z

ZOOMANCY   The art and practice of divination by observation of animal behavior (including reports of imaginary creatures such as sea serpents).

In medieval times, it was believed that the bansheelike howling of dogs portended death and calamities. A bat, pigeon, or robin redbreast that flew into the house was supposed to be an evil omen, as well as the flight of swallows or jackdaws down the chimney. If an owl showed itself in the sunlight, it meant bad luck. If one flew up against a window at night, it was an omen that a member of that family would soon die.

In the Victorian era, it was believed by many that a hare running through the town was a sure sign that someone there would soon be visited by fire.

In parts of the world where earthquakes often occur, the shaking of the ground is almost always presaged by the abnormal actions of animals, fish, and birds. (Diviners believe that this phenomena is due to the psychic sensitivity that all animals naturally possess.)

The drawing of earthquake or weather omens by unusual animal behavior (such as leaping fish, rearing horses, and panicked birds) originated in China, and it continues to be practiced in modern times.

An old woodcut portraying sailors on a ship being attacked by a gigantic sea serpent. The sightings of such creatures, as well as other supernatural monsters, were at one time believed by diviners who practiced zoomancy to be significant omens. In modern times, however, the behavior of ordinary mammals, fish, and birds are considered to be a prophetic indicator by diviners who practice the art. (Bettmann Archive)

Further Reading

Astrology

Astarte. *Astrology Made Easy*. North Hollywood, California: Wilshire Book Company, 1969.

De Vore, Nicholas. *Encyclopedia of Astrology*. New York: Philosophical Library, 1947.

Green, Landis Knight. *The Astrologer's Manual*. New York: Arco Publishing Company, 1975.

Leek, Sybil. *Moon Signs: Lunar Astrology*. New York: Berkley Publishing Corporation, 1977.

Leo, Alan. Edited by Vivian E. Robson. *The Complete Dictionary of Astrology*. New York: Astrologer's Library, 1978.

Parker, Derek and Julia. *The Compleat Astrologer*. New York: McGraw-Hill Book Company, 1971.

Rogers-Gallagher, Kim. *Astrology for the Light Side of the Brain*. San Diego, California: ACS Publications, 1995.

Sakoian, Frances and Louis Acker. *The Astrologer's Handbook*. New York: Harper and Row, 1973.

Sepharial. *New Dictionary of Astrology*. New York: Arco Publishing Company, 1964.

Wilson, James. *The Dictionary of Astrology*. York Beach, Maine: Samuel Weiser, 1974.

Woolfolk, Joanna Martine. *The Only Astrology Book You'll Ever Need*. Lanham, Maryland: Scarborough House, 1990.

Oneiromancy

Bethards, Betty. *The Dream Book: Symbols for Self-Understanding.* Petaluma, California: Inner Light Press, 1983.

Buckland, Raymond. *Secrets of Gypsy Dream Reading.* Saint Paul, Minnesota: Llewellyn Publications, 1990.

Dunwich, Gerina. *The Wicca Spellbook.* New York: Citadel Press, 1994.

Garfield, Patricia. *Healing Power of Dreams.* New York: Fireside Books, 1991.

Gibson, Walter B. and Litzka R. Gibson. *The Complete Illustrated Book of the Psychic Sciences.* New York: Pocket Books, 1966.

Morrison, Sarah Lyddon. *Modern Witch's Dreambook.* Secaucus, New Jersey: Citadel Press, 1990.

Schwartz, Alvin. *Telling Fortunes: Love Magic, Dreams, Signs, and Other Ways to Learn the Future.* New York: J.B. Lippincott, 1987.

Ullman, M., editor. *Dream Telepathy.* New York: Macmillan, 1973.

Tarot

Abraham, Sylvia. *How to Read the Tarot.* St. Paul, Minnesota: Llewellyn Publications, 1994.

Almond, Jocelyn, and Keith Seddon. *Understanding Tarot.* London: Aquarian Press, 1991.

Carlson, Laura E. *The Tarot Unveiled: The Method to Its Magic.* Stamford, Connecticut: U.S. Games Systems, 1988.

Cavendish, Richard. *The Tarot.* New York: Crescent Books, 1975.

Giles, Cynthia. *The Tarot: History, Mystery, and Lore.* New York: Paragon House, 1992.

Godwin, David. *How to Choose Your Own Tarot.* St. Paul, Minnesota: Llewellyn Publications, 1995.

Gordon, Richard, with Dixie Taylor. *The Intuitive Tarot: A Metaphysical Approach to Reading the Tarot Cards*. Nevada City, California: Blue Dolphin Publishing, 1994.

Hollander, P. Scott. *Tarot for Beginners*. St. Paul, Minnesota: Llewellyn Publications, 1995.

Konraad, Sandor. *Classic Tarot Spreads*. West Chester, Pennsylvania: Whitford Press, 1985.

Torres, Katherine. *Tarot: A Pathway to the Spirit Within*. Carlsbad, California: Earth People Medicine Publishers, 1994.

Waite, Arthur Edward. *The Pictorial Key to the Tarot*. Secaucus, New Jersey: University Books, 1995.

Tasseography

Buckland, Raymond. *Secrets of Gypsy Fortune Telling*. St. Paul, Minnesota: Llewellyn Publications, 1988.

Dunwich, Gerina. *The Wicca Spellbook*. Secaucus, New Jersey: Citadel Press, 1994.

Leland, Charles Godfrey. *Gypsy Sorcery and Fortune Telling*. New York: University Books, 1962.

McCrite, Harriet Mercedes. *Tea Leaf Reading Symbols*. Carlsbad, California: McCrite, 1991.

Selected Bibliography

Ashley, Leonard: *The Amazing World of Superstition, Prophecy, Luck, Magic, and Witchcraft* (Bell, New York, 1988).

Brasch, R.: *Strange Customs: How Did They Begin?* (David McKay Company, Inc. New York, 1976).

Cheiro: *Cheiro's Palmistry For All* (Arco Publishing, New York, 1982).

Drury, Nevill: *Dictionary of Mysticism and the Occult* (Harper and Row, New York, 1985).

Dunwich, Gerina: *The Concise Lexicon of the Occult* (Citadel Press, Secaucus, New Jersey, 1990).

Dunwich, Gerina: *Wicca Craft* (Citadel Press, Secaucus, New Jersey, 1991).

Dunwich, Gerina: *The Wicca Spellbook* (Citadel Press, Secaucus, New Jersey, 1994).

Eliot, Alexander: *Myths* (McGraw-Hill Book Company [UK] Limited, Maidenhead, England, 1976).

Gibson, Walter B. and Litzka R. Gibson: *The Complete Illustrated Book of the Psychic Sciences* (Pocket Books, New York, 1966).

Guiley, Rosemary Ellen: *The Encyclopedia of Witches and Witchcraft* (Facts on File, New York, 1989).

Guiley, Rosemary Ellen: *Harper's Encyclopedia of Mystical and Paranormal Experience* (Harper San Francisco, a division of Harper-Collins Publishers, New York, 1991).

Leach, Maria and Jerome Fried, editors: *Funk and Wagnalls Standard Dictionary of Folklore, Mythology and Legend* (Harper and Row, New York, 1984).

Levine, Frederick G.: *The Psychic Sourcebook: How to Choose and Use a Psychic* (Warner Books, New York, 1988).

Loewe, Michael and Carmen Blacker: *Oracles and Divination* (Shambhala, Boulder, Colorado, 1981).

Logan, Daniel: *The Anatomy of Prophecy* (Prentice-Hall, Inc., Englewood Cliffs, New Jersey, 1975).

Mysteries of Mind, Space and Time—The Unexplained (Volume 6): H.S. Stuttman, Inc. Westport, Connecticut, 1992 (originally published in the United Kingdom in weekly parts as *"The Unexplained"*).

Mysteries of the Unknown: Visions and Prophecies (Time-Life Books, Inc. Richmond, Virginia, 1988).

Opie, Iona and Moira Tatem: *A Dictionary of Superstitions* (Oxford University Press, Oxford, 1989).

Rawcliffe, D.H.: *Occult and Supernatural Phenomena* (Dover Publications, Inc. New York, 1987. Originally published by Derricke Ridgway Publishing Company Ltd. in 1952 under the title: *The Psychology of the Occult*).

Sarnoff, Jane and Reynold Ruffins: *Take Warning! A Book of Superstitions* (Charles Scribners' Sons, New York, 1978).

Schwartz, Alvin: *Telling Fortunes: Love Magic, Dreams, Signs, and Other Ways to Learn the Future* (J.B. Lippincott, New York, 1987).

Waite, Arthur Edward: *The Pictorial Key to the Tarot* (University Books, Secaucus, New Jersey, 1995).

Wilson, Joyce: *The Complete Book of Palmistry* (Bantam Books, New York, 1971).

Zolar: *Zolar's Encyclopedia of Ancient and Forbidden Knowledge* (Prentice-Hall, New York, 1986).

Cross Reference Guide

Accidental events   Transataumancy
Air and atmospheric phenomena   Aeromancy
Animals (behavior)   Zoomancy
Animals (chance meeting)   Apantomancy
Arrows   Belomancy
Ashes   Tephramancy
Astrological charts   Astro-Divination, Horoscopy
Automatic writing   Psychography
Auras   Auramancy
Axes or hatchets   Axiomancy
Barley leaf or cakes   Alphitomancy
Beasts   Theriomancy
Bible   Bibliomancy, Lots of the Saints
Birds   Augury, Ornithomancy
Black hen or rooster   Alectryomancy
Blood   Hemomancy
Books   Bibliomancy, Chartomancy, Rhapsodomancy
Brass vessels   Cattabomancy, Chalcomancy
Breastbone   Sternomancy
Brizo (goddess)   Brizomancy
Bulls   Tarbfeis
Candles   Lychnomancy
Cards   Cartomancy
Cats   Felidomancy
Caul   Amniomancy

143

Cheese   Tiromancy
Cinders or soot   Spodomancy
Clouds   Nephelomancy
Crystals   Crystalomancy
Death, corpses, spirits of the dead   Necromancy
Demons   Demonomancy
Dice   Astragalomancy, Astragyromancy
Divining rods   Dowsing
Dots (on paper at random)   Art of the Little Dots
Dreams and nightmares   Oneiromancy, Omen Dream
Dress   Stolisomancy
Dust   Abacomancy
Earth   Geomancy
Eggs   Oomantia, Ovamancy
Eyes   Oculomancy
Facial features   Physiognomy, Somatomancy
Feet   Podomancy
Fig leaves   Sycomancy
Fingernails   Onychomancy, Onyomancy
Fire   Causimomancy, Pyromancy
Fish   Ichthyomancy
Flowers   Floral Oracle, Floromancy, Phyllorhodomancy
Forehead   Metoposcopy
Fortune cookies   Aleuromancy
Foxes   Vulpesomancy
Frankincense   Livanomancy
Gazing   Scrying
Hands and fingers   Cheirognomy
Handwriting   Graphology, Psychographology
Herbs (esp. vervain)   Botanomancy
Homer   Homeric Lots
Horses   Hippomancy
Incense   Libanomancy

Intestines (human)   ANTHROPOMANCY, SPLANCHOMANCY
Intestines (animal)   HARUSPICY
Keys   CLEIDOMANCY
Knives, swords, etc.   MACHAROMANCY
Lamps   LAMPADOMANCY
Laughter   GELOSCOPY
Laurel branches   DAPHNOMANCY
Lead   MOLYBDOMANCY
Liver (of sheep)   HEPATOSCOPY
Logarithms   LOGARITHMANCY
Lots   CLEROMANCY, LOT-CASTING
Men's souls, etc.   PSYCHOMANCY
Mesmerism   METAGNOMY
Meteors and comets   METEOROMANCY
Mice and rats   MYOMANCY
Mirrors   CATOPTROMANCY
Moles (on body)   MOLEOSCOPY
Moon   SELENOMANCY
Names   CANCELLATION, ONOMANCY, ONOMANTICS, ONOMATOMANCY
Navel   OMPHILOMANCY
Numbers   ARITHMANCY, GEMATRIA, NUMEROLOGY
Oak tree and mistletoe   DENDROMANCY
Onion sprouts   CROMNIOMANCY
Oracles   CHRESMOMANCY
Palms   CHEIROMANCY, PALMISTRY
Pearls   MARGARITOMANCY
Pebbles   PESSOMANCY
Pendulum   CLEIDOMANCY, DACTYLOMANCY, RADIESTHESIA
Planetary influences   ASTROLOGY, ASTROMANCY, GENETHLIALOGY
Poetry or song lyrics   RHAPSODOMANCY
Prayer beads ("mala")   MO
Psychic impressions from objects   PSYCHOMETRY
Roses   PHYLLORHODOMANCY

Rounds or circles   GYROMANCY
Sacrificial offerings   HIEROMANCY
Salt   ALOMANCY
Shadows   SCIOMANCY
Shields   ASPIDOMANCY
Shoulder bone   ARMOMANCY
Sieves   COSCINOMANCY
Skin, bones, and excrements   SPATALAMANCY
Skull (ass or goat)   CEPHALOMANCY
Skull (human head)   PHRENOLOGY
Smoke   CAPNOMANCY
Snakes, serpents   OPHIOMANCY
Spirits   NECROMANCY, SEANCE, THEOMANCY
Stars   ROADOMANCY
Stones   LITHOMANCY
Straws   SIDEROMANCY
Sun and solar eclipses   HELIOMANCY
Tarot cards   CARTOMANCY, TAROTOLOGY
Tea leaves   TASSEOGRAPHY
Tests of endurance   ORDEALS
Thimbles   CUBOMANCY
Thunder and lightning   CERAUNOSCOPY
Urine   UROMANCY
Virgil   VIRGILIAN LOTS
Volcanoes   VULCANOSCOPY
Wands   RHABDOMANCY
Water   CYLICOMANCY, HYDATOSCOPY, HYDROMANCY, HYDROMANTIA
Wax   CEROMANCY
Wheel of fortune   CYCLOMANCY
Wind   AUSTROMANCY
Wine   OENOMANCY, OINOMANCY
Wood (twigs, branches, etc.)   XYLOMANCY